"Bill Greenway wants to awaken us to a primordial love that draws us into relationships of care for all creatures. Along the way he offers a valuable critique of modernity's scient*ism* and rational*ism* that drains the universe of mystery and ensconces the human as the sole locus of worth among all things. Arguing for a moral realism grounded in *agape*, Greenway offers us a *moral* vision of the infinite value of every creature that can, in turn, inform human *ethical* decision-making and action at a time when so much life on Earth is endangered."

—TIMOTHY H. ROBINSON

Lunger Associate Professor of Spiritual Resources and Disciplines, Brite Divinity School

"In *Agape Ethics*, Greenway skillfully engages philosophy, theology, ethics, and moral reasoning in a work that wades into the complex world in which we find ourselves: evermore aware of the beauty and complexity of the planet's eco-systems and inhabitants, while also aware of the difficult ethical challenges facing us as human actions threaten the planetary community. Williams' enlivening prose invites the reader in, equipping the reader with the tools to think morally and act ethically while embracing all creatures with love and gratitude. It is an important contribution between philosophy and theology, illuminating how to ethically and spiritually take our place as fellow creatures on the planet."

—LAUREL D. KEARNS

co-author of *Eco-Spirit: Theologies and Philosophies for the Earth*; Associate Professor, Drew Theological School

Agape Ethics

AGAPE ETHICS
Moral Realism and Love for All Life

William Greenway

CASCADE Books • Eugene, Oregon

AGAPE ETHICS
Moral Realism and Love for All Life

Copyright © 2016 William Greenway. All rights reserved. Except for brief quotations in critical publications or reviews, no part of this book may be reproduced in any manner without prior written permission from the publisher. Write: Permissions, Wipf and Stock Publishers, 199 W. 8th Ave., Suite 3, Eugene, OR 97401.

Cascade Books
An Imprint of Wipf and Stock Publishers
199 W. 8th Ave., Suite 3
Eugene, OR 97401

www.wipfandstock.com

PAPERBACK ISBN: 978-1-4982-0238-1
HARDCOVER ISBN: 978-1-4982-8613-8
EBOOK ISBN: 978-1-4982-0239-8

Cataloguing-in-Publication data:

Names: Greenway, William.

Agape ethics : moral realism and love for all life. / William Greenway.

Description: Eugene, OR: Cascade Books, 2016 | Includes bibliographical references.

Identifiers: ISBN 978-1-4982-0238-1 (paperback) | ISBN 978-1-4982-8613-8 (hardcover) | ISBN 978-1-4982-0239-8 (ebook)

Subjects: LCSH: 1. Animal welfare—Moral and ethical aspects. | 2. Agape. | 3. Ethics. | I. Title.

Classification: BT746 .G75 2016 (paperback) | CALL NUMBER (ebook)

Manufactured in the U.S.A.   12/08/16

New Revised Standard Version Bible, copyright 1989, Division of Christian Education of the National Council of the Churches of Christ in the United States of America. Used by permission. All rights reserved.

For Cindy and Kiki

Contents

Acknowledgements | ix

Introduction | 1

Part One: Awakening and Agape

Chapter 1
Love Diminished, Love Betrayed | 11

Chapter 2
Morality Diminished, Morality Betrayed | 24

Chapter 3
A Spirit Not Quite Lost: Rekindling the Spark | 36

Part Two: Science, Scientism, Morality

Chapter 4
Science not Scientism | 53

Chapter 5
Excursus On the Illusion of an Argument:
Daniel Dennett's *Consciousness Explained* | 65

Chapter 6
Affirming Science *and* Moral Realism | 76

Part Three—Beyond Objectivity, Relativism, and Extremism: Moral Realism, Ethical Surety, and the Sanctity of Life

Chapter 7
Against Ethical Relativism | 87

Chapter 8
Against Ethical Extremism | 100

Chapter 9
All Life is Sacred | 110

Part Four—Perfect Love in an Imperfect World: Agape Ethics

Chapter 10
Moral Sensitivity, Ethical Judgment, Ethical Conviction | 125

Chapter 11
Comparing Incomparables: Killing Nonhuman Creatures | 136

Bibliography | 145

Acknowledgements

This book has been more than a decade in the making, and over that period of time I have received support and encouragement from many people. My thanks to trustees, colleagues, students, and alumni of Austin Presbyterian Theological Seminary, who have cultivated a vital atmosphere of critical and open inquiry, and fostered commitments to justice and formation of loving communities. The poet and nature writer Jack Leax and, most especially, the noted Hebrew Bible scholar Patrick Miller have been continual sources of support. Author and respected editor Jana Reiss read the first chapters of this project many years ago and gave vital encouragement and important advice. I am thankful to all the people at Cascade Books at Wipf and Stock Publishers, who have been encouraging and flexible in the long process of getting this book into print, most especially to Rodney Clapp, Brian Palmer, and Matthew Wimer. This book also opened up a new path to substantial discussions with a longtime friend and former professor, the noted social ethicist Peter Paris, and I am especially grateful for his advice about, enthusiasm for, and willingness to endorse this project.

Many ideas in this book were worked out in lectures at churches and conferences, and three deserve special mention. First, the loving and dedicated people at Village Presbyterian Church, Prairie Village, Kansas, who invited me to deliver the 2010 Meneilly Lectures. Second, the stimulating, inquisitive, and learned students and faculty at Logsdon School of Theology and Hardin Simmons University, Abilene, Texas, who invited me to deliver the 2009 George Knight Lectures. Third, the passionate and learned scholars at the Oxford Centre for Animal Ethics, St. Stephens House, Oxford, where I delivered and benefitted from discussion of my 2014 lecture, "Peter Singer, Emmanuel Levinas, and Christian Agape: The Spiritual Heart of Animal Liberation."

Acknowledgements

I want to take this opportunity to thank also people whose influence upon this work has been more indirect but nonetheless significant, people who have through their care, generosity, and insight definitively enriched my life and shaped my understanding. First and foremost, my thanks to Bishop Hilario Gomez, Bishop Lorenzo Genotiva, Cobbie Palm, and all the wonderful people of the United Church of Christ of the Philippines (UCCP), especially all the people of the UCCP congregation on Abellanosa Street in Cagayan de Oro, Mindanao, and to all those in what was the "under the bridge community" at Barangay 17, all of whom were hosts, teachers, friends, and fellow workers for a critically formative year of ministry in 1989–1990.

Second, thanks to Professor D. T. Banda and the Reverend Monica Banda, Professors Lameck Banda, Victor Chilenje, Paul and Nolipher Moyo, Rian Venter, and all the faculty, students, and staff at Justo Mwale Theological University College, and also to Dean Elna Mouton, Professor Nico Koopman, and all the faculty of theology at Stellenbosch University, South Africa, all of whom, in Lusaka, Zambia, in Stellenbosch, South Africa, and as students and visiting lecturers in Austin, Texas, have been insightful colleagues and fellow inquirers, and who have provided hospitality and insight to me and my students.

Finally, my warm thanks to the Papendieck family—Jann and Brigitte, and their children Johannes and Karo—of Koblenz, Germany (one of Austin's sister cities), who so generously hosted my son and myself in their home for two wonderful weeks of an exchange program for elementary school students.

This book is dedicated to my wife, Cynthia (Cindy) L. Rigby, W. C. Brown Professor of Theology at Austin Presbyterian Theological Seminary, a widely admired professor, lecturer, and minister in the Presbyterian Church (USA), a longtime columnist on religion and public life for *The Dallas Morning News*, an expert on the intersections of theology, feminist theory, and society, and a continual source of support and inspiration. Together with Cindy, this book is dedicated to the first cat to adopt us, forming many years ago the first of what by now have been multiple iterations of our family, the loving, insightful, and faithful Kiki.

William Greenway
Winter 2016

Introduction

Kiki was the first cat to adopt my wife Cindy and me. We had just moved into a new house, and Kiki lived across the street. She was cautious. First no closer than fifteen feet, then ten, then five . . . and before we knew it she was insisting on spending all day in our house before we would send her home for the night. She was an older cat in a house full of young animals. She couldn't keep up and she was getting weaker, so she mounted a relentless argument through sheer presence for moving in. No matter how early, every morning when we came down the stairs from the bedroom there would be Kiki, crammed up on the tiny outside ledge of the window beside the front door, meowing insistently until we let her in for the day.

Finally, Kiki won her argument. The folks across the street agreed she had decided to move in with us. Kiki knew it right away, too, when we didn't put her out before locking the door for the night. I had never seen her so full of energy. To celebrate, we got out a big marshmallow and let her chase it around on the kitchen floor. Finally we went up to bed, leaving Kiki downstairs in the kitchen with her marshmallow. Cindy got up first the next morning, stepped into the upstairs hallway, laughed, and called me out. In the upstairs hall was a laundry basket full of clean clothes. Curled up in the basket, sound asleep, was Kiki. Beside her in the basket was her marshmallow.

* * * * *

I was at the Austin-Bergstrom International Airport when I saw a cricket on the floor near my gate. I got the cricket to settle onto my bag, but I realized that I could only get it outside by going all the way back out of the airport. With my flight about to depart, I clearly did not have time to release the cricket outside, get back through security ,and still make my plane. I felt bad, since the cricket was stuck inside. But I decided I would have to let it fend for itself. I thought there was a pretty good chance it would find its way home. Asking a friend to watch my bag, I walked away to buy a snack. When I returned the cricket was nowhere to be found.

As I was boarding the plane I heard a woman shout out, "It's a cricket!" Evidently, the cricket had hidden in a fold of my backpack. I had reached the end of the Jetway leading out from the gate to the door of the plane. There is always a gap where the Jetway meets the side of the plane, the gap where one can peek out at the outside of the airplane. When I got to that gap to the outdoors the cricket had seen his chance and he had taken it. I looked down and saw where he had landed alongside the opening to the outside. He did a little jump-turn to face the opening. "Get it," she yelled as she stretched her body forward and stamped down her foot, crushing the cricket.

This is a reflexive reaction among Western adults to bugs of all sorts. What sort of spirit reacts this way, even to the life of a cricket? I was stunned and genuinely uncomprehending. I didn't say anything, but she saw my face. Because I was so clearly not mad or attacking, but shocked and saddened, she was not defensive. She looked a bit surprised, perhaps even a bit ashamed. She seemed suddenly to realize what she had done to that cricket, and to herself.

* * * * *

In this book I take happiness for Kiki and sorrow over the cricket with absolute seriousness. I argue that such responses unveil a primordial truth about the ultimate character of reality, namely, a truth about the reality of agape and its all-inclusive reach. Modern Westerners are largely aware of the reality and reach of agape, but this truth, a truth at the heart of the very meaningfulness of existing, has been wrenched out of focus by powerful conceptual trajectories in modern Western thought.

For instance, people give dogs, cats, horses, birds, and other nonhuman creatures, even plants, personal names; they communicate with them, feed them, live with them, play with them, and look to them for companionship. They care for them when they are ill, take joy in their delights, wonder at their beauty, and grieve them when they die. They also eat them and wear them and experiment on them, often all in the same day. People

Introduction

live these deep conflicts daily. These conflicts are, once named, obvious. Yet in modern Western society these conflicts remain largely unnamed and buried to conscious acknowledgement.

Not only nonhuman animals are harmed when we fail to name and address these conflicts. This is far more than an issue of animal rights. Humans too are harmed by human-centered and love-negating conceptual trajectories that are carried in predominant streams of modern Western rationality. Many Westerners live in denial of an essential and essentially good dimension of reality, alienated not only from a moral dimension of reality but also from a spiritual dimension of their own being.

The good news is that most people truly have been seized by care and concern for other creatures, human and nonhuman. Though most people are to a significant degree morally awake, most never bring to consciousness the deep conflicts they live. Perhaps they just cannot bear to acknowledge the amount of suffering they would have to endure if they named the suffering of all creatures.

I have a friend, a passionate and committed relief worker who has lent critical aid to thousands of hurting people. She heard me present some of the material from this book at a conference. In a private moment after the presentation, my friend said to me, "I deal with so much pain and suffering among people every day that if I had to admit the suffering of all animals it would just be too much." That is understandable. But since clearly she realizes the moral truth about the suffering of all creatures, there is no chance her attempt to shut it out of her mind and deny it will give her peace. To the contrary, since she does not believe the denial, since she needs to make an effort to deny, such denial is harmful not only to other creatures but also to her and her own spiritual well-being.

Acknowledging complicity in causing suffering can be difficult, even traumatic. Nobel Peace Prize Laureate and medical missionary Albert Schweitzer acknowledged that if one is honest with oneself about these conflicts, if one has reverence for *all* life, then existence will "become harder . . . in every respect than it would be if one lived for oneself." But, he urges, "at the same time it will be richer, more beautiful, and happier. It will become, instead of mere living, a real experience of life."[1]

Insofar as we reflexively kill crickets, insofar as we do not take joy in the tale of Kiki, insofar as we remain closed off from love for *all* creatures, we are alienated from moral reality and the meaningfulness of life. For love,

---

1. Schweitzer, *Out of My Life and Thought*, 268.

love in the sense of altruism or agape, lies at the heart of moral reality, and agape opens us to the most profound and meaningful dimensions of reality.

Major streams of modern Western rationality, however, reject the very idea of agape. Thereby modern Western rationality alienates us from agape, from moral reality, from all other creatures, from joy, fellowship, sorrow, and sadness, from "a real experience of life." The world is disenchanted, hollowed out. We are left with a cold vision of atomistic egos pursuing individual desires for pleasure, security, and power in a war of all against all.

Fortunately, this devastating vision is not only diminished and depressing, it is incorrect. In this book I argue for reawakening to the moral dimension of reality, reawakening to agape, reawakening to having been seized by love for every creature, for every Kiki, every cricket, and every human.[2] I strive to identify and clear away modern Western conceptual obstacles that alienate us from moral reality, obstacles that cut us off from having been seized by love for all creatures (i.e., from agape). I strive to articulate the dynamics and implications of awakening to having been seized by love. These are especially pertinent first steps in a modern Western context for, I will argue, modern Western philosophy, science, and Christian theology, despite their many wonderful gifts, have in significant ways cut us off from spiritual reality, cut us off from spiritual communion with other creatures, and cut us off from spiritual delight in all creation.[3]

Predominant modern Western conceptual trajectories (and these trajectories now have global influence) impede us from naming, affirming, and owning our having been seized by love for all creatures. This is a devastating loss. I join an increasingly vibrant and critical struggle—happily, books, essays and general interest in this topic is exploding—to reawaken

---

2. As I will explain in detail below, I use the admittedly cumbersome formula "having been seized by love" for the sake of precision. In particular, I use it in contrast to two other possible and predominant ways of thinking about the sources of our attitudes/emotions/intentions, namely, that they are either a product of our choice/intention or they are a product of the way we have been programmed to respond by nature and/or nurture. I will contend that loving, agapic relation to others is neither a product of our decision/choice nor determined by nature/nurture programming, for it is prior to our choice/intention on the one hand, but a dynamic we can choose to resist on the other (i.e., we can harden our hearts). In other words, for instance, I neither choose to care for Kiki and the cricket, nor do I find myself helplessly fated to care for them, rather, at the critical moment of encounter I find myself already seized by them, and yet still free to harden my heart towards them.

3. Insofar as I discuss faith traditions I will focus upon Christian theology (an area in which I possess expertise), but analogous problems can be discerned across modern faith traditions.

Introduction

us to a lost source of spiritual comfort and joy, to reawaken us to moral reality, to reawaken us to a lost sense of spiritual belonging in this world, and to retrieve a lost sense of communion with all creatures and all creation.

Awakening is often decisively stimulated in reaction to moral violation, where the reality of the moral can bear down upon us with incredible power. So I dream that on the day that woman crushed the cricket at the airport, and then saw her action through the shocked and pained eyes of another, that on that day she experienced the beginning of true enlightenment. I dream that today that woman saves crickets and knows the joy of awakening, the intense joy of having been seized by love for all creatures.

The hope that that woman may have been awakened by the moral reality so powerfully manifest in the crushing of the cricket, however, does nothing to mitigate the awful, final, and irremediable murder of that cricket. There is no gainsaying the ongoing reality of suffering and evil in our world. The temptation to denial in the face of all the suffering and evil can be powerful. But while the temptation to denial is powerful, denial depends upon profound spiritual alienation. So my argument will remain awake to painful dimensions of existence, even though unblinking awakening delivers not only joy but also sorrow.

* * * * *

I unfold the argument in four parts. In the first part, "Awakening and Agape," I strive to stimulate spiritual awakening by invoking and affirming the reality of our love for all creatures while unmasking systemic distortions in modern Western rationality that alienate us from that love and from nonhuman creatures. I argue that loving reaction to Kiki and the cricket is revelatory of a primordial truth about reality, the truth of agape, a truth that anchors moral realism, unveils the meaningfulness of life, and explains the poignancy of life and of ethical reflection in a far from perfect world. In particular, I explain pertinent aspects of the thought of renowned philosopher Emmanuel Levinas, whose talk of "awakening" I appropriate, and whose reflections on being seized by the faces of others are pivotal for my unfolding of the reality and all-inclusive reach of agape.[4]

The second part of the argument, "Moral Realism in a Secular Age," continues and enhances a criticism of an especially unfortunate aspect of

---

4. For detailed argument for the reality of agape, see Greenway, *A Reasonable Belief*, 77–120.

mainstream modern Western rationality, namely, its dismissal of moral realism and agape. I complete my defense of moral realism and agape in this second part of the argument and, just as importantly, since I want to affirm many aspects of modern Western rationality, most especially modern Western science, I explain how we can affirm both moral realism *and* modern science.

By the end of the second part of the argument my defense of agape and moral realism is complete. At this point, however, some challenges become visible. I reawaken us to moral passions while rejecting the appeals to objectivity that modern Western thought used to curb ethical and religious enthusiasm. This has the virtue of returning agape to the heart of ethics and anchoring moral realism. Rejecting objective ethical reasoning, however, resurrects the specters of relativism and extremism. Accordingly, in the third part, "Beyond Objectivity, Relativism, and Extremism: Moral Realism and Ethical Surety," I respond to these dangers by explaining how we can address the challenges of moral extremism and moral relativism.

Another challenge springs from the origins of my argument in awakening to love for Kiki and the cricket, for the reality of this love erases the bright moral line commonly drawn between humans and other creatures. Accordingly, in the fourth part, "Perfect Love in an Imperfect World: Agape Ethics," I attempt to sketch out ethical principles for use in contexts where infinite love for every creature must be compromised when one is caught in situations in which inevitably one creature or another will be harmed. I distinguish between the *moral*, which names awakening to agape and thereby to the infinite worth of every creature, and the *ethical*, which names reflection upon the question of what is the best action when all of one's forced live options involve degrees of violation of agape (i.e., degrees of evil). For instance, I explain why, if one were confronted with a real life-and-death forced decision between saving a cat and a human boy, one *should* save the boy *and* mourn the cat. Finally, in relation to the question of when it would be *ethical* (not good, but the best among bad options) for a human to kill a deer, I attempt to sketch out general ethical principles in light of awakening to the primordial truth of love for all creatures (i.e., I sketch the general principles of agape ethics in relation to the killing of a deer).

While I do not develop a full-scale technical analysis in explicit conversation with other ethicists, I believe the approach I develop here, inspired above all by Emmanuel Levinas, addresses a quiet crisis in modern ethics, where there is currently not only no consensus regarding first principles,

Introduction

but widespread skepticism regarding moral reality. The proposal I develop here is hardly new. Indeed, it is ancient: what essential reality lies at the heart of morality and yields the very meaningfulness of life? Love.

This book is for all who seek to perfect their love for every creature and their delight in all creation. It joins a rapidly growing collection of works that strive to overcome a tragic, deadening alienation that harms creation and its many creatures, an alienation that wounds our spirits, robbing us of wellsprings of vitality and joy. It strives to reawaken love for every Kiki and every cricket. While never forgetting all the suffering and cruelty suffusing reality, it strives to reawaken people to love, joy, and delight in creation. I strive to do this out of love for all creatures—including creatures who can read and reflect ethically. For, as Schweitzer realized, while existence lived in the light of awakening to love for all creatures will "become harder . . . in every respect than it would be if one lived for oneself," at the same time it will be "richer, more beautiful, and happier. It will become, instead of mere living, a real [and, I will be arguing, a *more true, loving, and good*] experience of life."[5]

---

5. Schweitzer, *Out of My Life and Thought*, 268.

Part One

AWAKENING AND AGAPE

Chapter 1

Love Diminished, Love Betrayed

A MODERN FABLE ABOUT PRIDE AND DISCOVERY

Let me begin by considering a major way in which modern Western philosophy and science cuts us off from creation. In the seventeenth century, Rene Descartes—and he was by no means alone—helped us come to see the universe as a great machine working in accord with the laws of nature. We exempted only ourselves. All reality was divided into matter and spirit: "matter," the insensitive realm of the machine, and "spirit," the realm of sentience, freedom, feeling, and value. In Descartes's view, which became standard for the next four centuries of modern Western thought, spirit exists only in humans.

The significance of this conceptual split for all creation and all creatures becomes clear when one sees how it is related to a popular understanding—a fable, really—about the conceptual revolution sparked by the brilliant scientific work of Descartes's contemporary, Galileo Galilei. The fable talks about how in the seventeenth century science humbled humanity, for science discovered that the earth revolves around the sun. In the medieval period people thought they were the center of the universe. They thought the universe revolved around them, and so they thought they had pride of place. Their place at the center of the cosmos fed their pride, so the fable goes, until science taught them that the universe does not revolve around them after all. So these people fought the humbling lessons of the new science. They even persecuted the truth tellers. Their pride at being at the center of the cosmos made them shameless and shameful.[1]

Now, it is most certainly true that Galileo was unjustly censured by the church and was wrongly subject to house arrest for the last years of his life. And it is also true that in the wake of Galileo's censure scientific inquiry in Italy withered. This injustice and its consequences should be named and remembered. Criticism of the fable should in no way lessen criticism of the church's treatment of Galileo. But the fable is not really about Galileo, let alone about the technical, mid-seventeenth-century debates in Europe over the relationship between natural philosophy (as natural science was then called) and theology. The fable is really about a shift in humanity's self-image and understanding of our place in the cosmos. With regard to that shift, the fable portrays a reality that is opposite to the truth.

According to the fable, the scientific revolution humbled human pride because it displaced humans from their exalted place at the center of the cosmos and revealed that humans were, after all, just another part of nature, inhabitants of a small planet circling an otherwise unremarkable star amidst a vast cosmos. In this critical respect, the fable is only trivially true. Physically, the scientific revolution of the seventeenth century displaced us from the center of the universe. But in the medieval, Aristotelian/Ptolemaic paradigm, the one the scientific revolution displaced, the center of the universe, where the earth was believed to be, far from being a place of pride was considered to be the worst place in the cosmos, below the perfect, ethereal realms of the moon, planets, and stars, at the furthest remove from God's heavenly home beyond the outermost sphere. We were caught near the pit of the cosmos, just above hell, which was at the very center of the cosmos. Earth was a degraded sphere of change, death, and decay. Our place near the center of the cosmos primarily reflected the base nature of our mortal existence.

Despite their humble location in the pit of the cosmos, people still found ways to see themselves as among the most important beings in creation. Humans asserted their significance *despite* their humble position at

---

1. We hear the standard fable, for instance, from Princeton bioethicist Peter Singer in *Rethinking Life and Death*: "[Copernicus] suggested that the planets, including the earth, revolve around the sun. This remarkable new view met with stiff resistance, because it required us to give up our cherished idea that we are the centre of the universe. It also clashed with the Judeo-Christian view of human beings as the pinnacle of creation" (187). This new view raised a very uncomfortable question, "If we are the reason why everything else was made, why do we have such an undistinguished address?" (ibid.).

the pit of the cosmos. We affirmed our significance, end, hope, and measure by placing ourselves within a larger context. We were sinful, mortal beings mired in the decaying sphere of the earth. True significance and hope, however, could be found insofar as we understood ourselves to be part of an order higher and greater than ourselves, an order founded in the Good and Eternal reality reflected in the ethereal spheres of the heavens, an order which ultimately oriented us to God.

We saw ourselves as by far the most important of mortal beings, then, but our significance was derivative, dependent upon the love and concern of the Holy and Loving One who resided in perfection beyond the outermost sphere, dependent upon the love and concern of God. We were not the measure of all things. We were mortal beings enmeshed in a larger physical, moral, and spiritual order. We *recognized* when we were moved by goodness, beauty, evil, and injustice.

By contrast, in the modern paradigm of the scientific revolution there is no center and no heavenly realm. No base realm below and ethereal realms above. All is machine. Or rather, all is machine but us. Humans alone are sentient, feeling, free, valuing. Only we are capable of moral consideration, only we have intrinsic value, only we warrant moral consideration, only we can be wronged, frustrated, violated, or denied fulfillment.

The popular scientific fable masks reality. In the scientific revolution humans were, trivially, displaced from the center of the universe. But philosophically, scientifically, and existentially, in the wake of the scientific revolution we alone rise above the brute flux of the material realm, we alone are self-aware and self-determining. The critical spiritual shift of the scientific revolution pivots not upon humans being displaced from the center of the cosmos, it pivots upon the destruction of the orienting moral matrix within which we interpreted our selves and our place within a larger whole.

Put otherwise, in the scientific revolution it was the external measure that was displaced. What was revolutionary and disturbing to contemporary theologians and to natural philosophers (i.e., scientists) alike—notably, many natural philosophers were also priests and virtually all were theists—was not that humans were displaced from the physical center of the cosmos, it was that God was displaced, along with the outermost sphere of heaven and along with the whole moral/cosmological order, only to be replaced with a self-same, mechanical universe operating blindly according to the inexorable laws of nature.

Part One: Awakening and Agape

In the wake of this shift Westerners came to see themselves not as living *within creation*, but as living *above nature*. They came to see their significance not as derivative, but as intrinsic, a function of their superiority over all animals and all of nature, for only humans possess mind (spirit). All else, everything other than human minds, is relegated to the insensate sphere of the mechanism, the sphere of matter, of things.

Contrary to the fable about our humbling, the new science combined with Descartes's human-centered division between "matter" (the insensitive realm of the machine, the quantifiable) and "spirit" (the realm of sentience, free will, feeling, and value) and became not an occasion for the humbling of humanity, but the basis for an assertion of human pride of place unimaginable within the medieval, Christianized Aristotelian/Ptolemaic cosmology. Existentially, we humans were radically loosed from our moorings within a created order now seen as brute flux. Within the world as modern Westerners came to see it, morally and existentially, *humans become the sole locus of value in the universe.*

According to the modern picture, human minds alone are the measure of anything and everything (for the sake of argument I leave aside the possible existence of extraterrestrials). Human minds are the only place where there is realization of any morals, beauty, or understanding. In the medieval paradigm humans were moral beings within a larger moral order that was ultimately subservient to God. In the modern paradigm humans are the only sources of value and valuing within a vast machine.

The scientific fable about the modern scientific humbling of humanity masks the reality of the momentous transition to the modern Western scientific image of existence: the emergence of humans as supreme beings, distinguished qualitatively and absolutely from all the rest of existence, which is now denigrated to the status of thing. Humans are de-centered only in a physical sense that, far from humbling, enables assertion of a previously unimaginable extreme of human pride. Humans become the sole measure of all things.[2]

---

2. For technical background on the shifts delineated here see, among others, Burtt, *Metaphysical Foundations of Modern Science*; Butterfield, *The Origins of Modern Science*; Brooke, *Science and Religion*; Dupre, *Passage to Modernity*; Grant, *Planets, Stars and Orbs*; Lindberg, *Beginnings of Western Science*; and Lindberg and Numbers, eds., *God and Nature*.

Love Diminished, Love Betrayed

GNOSTICISM AND MODERN "ORTHODOX" CHRISTIANITY

Most Christians (which is to say, in the West in the seventeenth and eighteenth centuries, most everyone) integrated this astounding pride theologically. Following Descartes and others, Christians pictured themselves as part spirit and part machine. In all of creation, Christians began to think, God is ultimately concerned only with our spirits. Not surprisingly, today the vast majority of the world's Christians, thinking themselves orthodox and even biblical, believe they have a soul and a body and when they die their souls will go to heaven while their bodies and the earth will perish.

Christian theology is not my focus, but it is worth pointing out that, in terms of Christianity's fidelity to its classic confessions, this modern soul/body perspective, with its vision of souls leaving bodies and ascending to heaven, is Gnostic. Let me pause here for a moment to explain what "Gnostic" names. Gnosticism names a Neoplatonic philosophy that was very influential in the Roman Empire in the first few centuries after the time of Jesus. It was an anti-physical philosophy that saw salvation in terms of escape from the physical into a purely spiritual realm.

The Gnostics, taking a cue from the Platonic idea that our ability to recognize eternal mathematical truths was evidence that a part of us was eternal, thought that each person was essentially a divine spark, now fallen and encased within a material body and world. Some Gnostics saw matter as evil, others as a benefit insofar as it encased divine sparks and kept us from falling even further from true, eternal, nonmaterial reality. In either case, the goal of the Gnostics was (perhaps over the course of many lifetimes) to ascend through a hierarchy of increasingly more perfect realms until we were purified of any traces of material existence, coarse desires, and so forth, and finally emerged, wholly purified, into perfect spiritual existence.

Obviously, the Gnostics took a dim view of the physical world. This was in marked contrast to classic Jewish theology, which thought that God created the world, celebrated its goodness, was interested in the earth and all creatures, and was working towards establishing a new heavens and new earth. The "heavens" of "a new heavens and a new earth" in this Hebrew and early Christian context is not a reference to some spiritual, otherworldly realm, but a reference to the realm of the planets and stars. "A new heavens and new earth" is another way of saying "a new cosmos," not *another* heavens and *another* earth, not a nonphysical realm, but a rejuvenation and renewal and perfecting of this cosmos, including its physical and its spiritual/moral/aesthetic dimensions. In the poetic words of the prophet Isaiah, the ancient Hebrews lived in hope and anticipation of the day when "the earth will be full of the knowledge of the Lord as the waters cover the sea."[3]

Gnosticism is also markedly different from Christianity. Christianity, precisely in the face of the contemporary dominance of Neoplatonic, anti-physical, sheerly escapist spiritualities and philosophies, remained committed to Judaism's ultimate affirmation of the profound significance of the physical world in its own signal proclamation that in Jesus Christ God Godself became flesh (i.e., the essence of Jesus and of God was *homoousion*, "of the same substance"). This affirmation is a continuation and radicalizing of the classic Jewish affirmation of God's profound passion for all of creation and all creatures. It is a kenotic, God's-love-descending affirmation that Christianity takes to an incredible, flesh-affirming extreme in its doctrine of incarnation, of the *homoousios*, of "the Word become flesh."[4] It is an affirmation made directly in the face of the escapist, otherworldly spirituality predominant in the contemporary Roman Empire.

As a result, Christian theology continued to describe the significance of Jesus Christ in classic Jewish terms, speaking of God's ultimate creation of a new heavens and new earth. Indeed, a definitive early Christian theological refrain, one which proved pivotal in the formation of classic Christian Christology, was "that which is not assumed is not redeemed," which stressed that not only the mental and spiritual but also the physical is "assumed" in the incarnation because not only the mental and the spiritual but also the physical is "redeemed."[5] This explains why the Christian Gospels emphasize a *bodily* resurrection and take care to paint a picture of a post-resurrection Jesus physically ascending into heaven. The Apostle Paul adds nuance by speaking cryptically of new bodies that have "put on immortality," but in any case, the emphasis is emphatically upon the worth of physical creation. By contrast, "Gnostic" names spiritualities that denigrate physical reality and seek salvation in total escape from any physical existence.

---

3. Isaiah 11:9 (*NRSV*).

4. John 1:14 (*NRSV*).

5. This quote from Gregory of Nazianzus is the standard shorthand reference to his influential critique of Apollinarius.

Love Diminished, Love Betrayed

To return to the key point with regard to Christianity, the modern soul/body perspective, with its vision of souls leaving bodies and ascending to heaven, is Gnostic. It is not biblical. It contradicts repeated biblical talk of a new heavens and a new earth. It is contrary to the classic doctrines of creation and incarnation. It involves a denial of the *homoousious*, of "the Word became flesh." It is a classic heresy explicitly condemned by the great ecumenical councils of the patristic period. And today it is a dominant Christian understanding even among Christians who think of themselves as classically orthodox. Moreover, the most significant proximate reason for this being today's dominant Christian understanding is modern Western Christianity's unwitting absorption of an Enlightenment split that renders the whole universe—including even our very bodies—machine, excepting only human minds (souls).

GNOSTICISM AND MODERN WESTERN RATIONALITY: A SYSTEMIC DISTORTION

Aside from and beyond Christianity, consider how a quietly but decisively Gnostic mentality structured mainstream Western scholarly reflection. Consider how knowledge is still organized in modern universities and, to a large extent, in modern Western rationality generally. It would not be uncommon to think of this organization as instituting a division between the natural and the human sciences. This would be largely correct, but importantly imprecise insofar as both of these are realms of science. A more precise organization would distinguish between *the realm of the sciences*, that is, the realm of the natural and human sciences, all of which treat their objects of study from a dispassionate perspective, and which involve objective, quantifiable, public, and publicly testable empirical claims, and *the realm of the humanities*, which demands passionate, subjective understanding, wherein judgments regarding degrees of excellence or deficiency cannot be pegged by publicly testable empirical claims but depend upon cultivated tastes and the wisdom of expert communities.

The natural and social sciences consider us insofar as we are kinds, types, susceptible to statistical analyses, objects whose future behavior will in theory fall into predictable patterns. Thus the natural and social sciences give considerable insight into how we behave and think as matters of fact, but cannot say how we should behave or think as matters of moral value. Social scientists can describe the character of various emotions, their typical context, frequency and impact upon behavior, but social scientists are not even attempting to communicate or generate the passionate in itself—to the contrary, the integrity of social scientists as social scientists quite rightly turns precisely upon them and their work remaining objective and dispassionate.

Notably, social scientists can also describe the ethical norms of a society and evaluate those norms' functionality vis-à-vis various outcomes (e.g., the likelihood of maximizing the endurance potential of the society, the likelihood of maximizing the productivity of the society, the likelihood of maximizing a society's "excellence" [however that is defined], the likelihood of maximizing individuals' "happiness" [typically indexed to pleasure]), but social scientists cannot see the moral in itself and are not even attempting to communicate or evaluate the reality of having been seized by love for others (i.e., moral reality). To the contrary, once again, the integrity of social scientists as social scientists quite rightly turns precisely upon them and their work remaining objective and dispassionate.

The humanities, by contrast, are involved in discerning, generating, enhancing, and evaluating subjective emotional, aesthetic, and moral states. Understanding in the humanities involves the ability to be taken up by a symphony, moved by a dance, or horrified by an injustice. In the humanities, an essential element of understanding is passionate, subjective involvement.

Now, what concerns me about this modern Western way of dividing up spheres of knowledge is the way in which it delimits legitimate ways of reflecting upon creation and nonhuman creatures. For this way of structuring knowledge perpetuates a systematic distortion that alienates us from creation and nonhuman creatures. Note first that under the domain of study of the natural and social sciences one finds things such as machines, matter, energy, social structures, social norms, political and legal systems, and human and nonhuman creatures—all visible and subject to study insofar as they appear empirically as types or kinds in brute determinate (and to some degree possibly indeterminate) causal relation with one another. Far more significantly, the domain of the humanities—the nonempirical realm where beauty and good and evil can appear—*typically includes only humans and artifacts of human creativity* such as literature, painting, or architecture.

Through this dominant structuring of reason not only in universities and scholarly investigations but throughout our educational system and Western rationality generally, Gnosticism, that is, moral and empathetic disregard for all nonhuman creatures, has been inscribed into modernity's dominant organization of knowledge. While this systemic distortion is now beginning to be overcome in Western institutions, it remains predominant. Insofar as it still structures reflection, nonhuman creatures either appear as objects within the domain of the sciences, or they do not appear at all. In sum, modern thought perpetuates a conceptual distortion that systematically renders all nonhuman creatures invisible as fellow subjects of love and concern.

As a result, if I attempt to understand an animal empathetically, that is, by accessing my own hopes, fears, joys, or pain in order to imagine the animal's hopes, fears, joys, or pain, then I am thought to be terribly confused. I am violating the boundaries of modern rationality, for I am wrongly applying human categories to animals. That's why in typical modern humanities classes in art, music, literature, or ethics you will study humans and their creative artifacts. But when it comes to cats and dogs and dolphins and horses, and to their nests and play and talk, you will almost certainly be in biology or ecology classes, where typically animals are either dissected or at best understood empirically in the context of some holistic system or another.

If, by contrast, someone reflects upon a dog or cat using the subjective, passionate categories of the humanities, they are typically reproached for being anthropomorphic, that is, for confusedly attributing to animals capacities that belong uniquely to humans. This was the norm that Jane Goodall was initially criticized for violating in her groundbreaking study of chimpanzees. Fortunately, while the anthropocentric approach still reigns, Goodall's approach is steadily gaining momentum in the broader scientific community, in particular under the now blossoming field that Donald Griffin christened "cognitive ethology."[6]

Notably, anthropomorphism was classically used to critique the attribution of human characteristics to God. This was seen as a problem because it belittled God. It was a crossing and compromising of a boundary that protected the otherness and holiness of God. In the modern context, anthropomorphism is used to critique the attribution of human characteristics to animals. This is seen as a problem because it belittles humans. It is a crossing and compromising of a boundary that protects the otherness and privilege of humans. The theological idea of a space qualitatively distinct from all creatures and all creation is retained. Now, after the scientific

---

6. See Griffin, *Animal Minds*, as well as the works of Marc Bekoff.

revolution, it is not God but *we humans* who are set apart from all other creatures and creation.

It is against this conceptual background that those who express love and concern for nonhuman animals have been branded and dismissed as silly, sentimental, unrealistic, and hopelessly romantic. A Gnostic mentality permeates not just modern Christianity but Western culture generally. In the wake of our so-called Enlightenment, the whole of creation and all creatures as a community of subjects almost wholly vanished from our philosophical and theological consciousness. In the predominant modern Western conceptual paradigm all nonhuman "life-forms," and all the rest of nature, including human bodies, came to be seen as part of a thing, as organic parts in a vast, variably organic and inorganic machine. Only human minds were exempted. In all existence, many modern Westerners came to believe, there are ultimately only two kinds of stuff: mind and matter. Mind is found only in humans, dotted about amidst a vast machine. In all existence all value and valuing is found in minds alone. We are the measure of all things.

This is one powerful way in which modern Western science and philosophy, for all their wonder and value, unintentionally but decisively diminished and betrayed human love for all creatures and all creation. This is how modern philosophy and science cut humans off from creation. This is in large part how the modern conceptual revolution—the scientific revolution, the Enlightenment, the Age of Reason—exactly contrary to the fable about the humbling of humanity, enabled a degree of human pride unimaginable in the medieval period. This historic and ongoing failing should be frankly named, or else humanity will remain vulnerable to the hubris of its supposed enlightenment, and as a result, human love for all creatures will continue to be a love diminished, a love betrayed.

Two tales about popular culture and animals

Let me close this chapter with two stories that made national news some years ago. I'm telling both from memory, but I'm not overly concerned about the precise details because they are irrelevant to my point and because both stories are of a familiar type and you will be able to bring many other examples to mind. The first story turned into a saga that filled the international news for a week or two at the end of the cold war in 1988 (in 2012 Universal Pictures turned the story into a Hollywood movie, *Big Miracle*,

Love Diminished, Love Betrayed

starring Drew Barrymore). Three whales were trapped in rapidly forming ice off the arctic coast of Alaska. Open water was only a few miles away but beyond the whales' reach. The whales were sharing a single shrinking air hole in the ice. Video showed the whales' spouts and sprays of seawater as they surfaced for air.

As the days passed, increasingly frigid temperatures repeatedly closed ice over the air hole. Working in shifts day and night, American rescuers repeatedly reopened the hole with axes and sledgehammers. Meanwhile, a Russian icebreaker, slowly breaking open a path through the ice, steamed to the rescue. Eventually, with workers now living on the ice in their struggle to keep the air hole open, the icebreaker succeeded in breaking a passage through several miles of ice, opening a clear passage to open water for the whales. Dependent upon that single small hole for nearly two weeks, the whales recognized the route to escape the second it opened up within range. Russian and American viewers, no doubt along with many others, smiled at video of exhausted but happy rescuers cheering the whales as they swam into the freedom of the open sea.

* * * * *

The second story, which made national news in the States, was about a seal who was trapped in an industrial outtake tank on the coast of California.[7] There was some sort of elevated boardwalk along the beach from which the tank could be seen, and soon someone had spotted the seal and realized its plight. By the time news crews arrived a rescue effort was underway. Guiding the seal back out to sea proved difficult. Workers struggled to help the increasingly desperate seal to escape. As the hours passed, a large crowd of families—moms, dads, and kids—gathered to cheer on the rescuers. Finally, to many smiles and happy cries, the rescuers managed to lead the seal through the correct passageways and free it into the open ocean. With fast bounds above water and dives beneath, the seal could be seen swimming excitedly out to sea. Still within sight, maybe seventy-five yards out, an orca banged up into view, slammed the seal into the air, caught it, and then submerged, the now limp seal hanging from its jaws.

---

7. I tell this story to make a similar point in a different context, namely, when discussing the love of all creatures in the primeval history in the book of Genesis (Greenway, *For the Love of All Creatures*, 127–32).

Part One: Awakening and Agape

* * * * *

While the sad ending of the second story is unusual, I take these to be familiar "rescue" story lines. One routinely finds stories like these—typically with happy endings—on the local and national news. This is in itself heartening. On the whole, despite the betrayals of modern Western rationality and the condescending and dismissive attitude many intellectuals still take to such stories, the fact is that the vast majority of people are moved when they see an animal in distress, they value efforts to save the animals, and they feel joy when the animal is rescued or freed. The pictures of smiling children clapping gleefully only makes more visible the inner feelings of more reserved adults. In this story the tears of those same children at the fate of the seal are just as real, though this time perhaps the children truly were more genuinely uncomprehending than the adults, whose hopes and expectations may well have been blunted through previous bitter experience.

Indeed, the bitterness of disappointed expectations can lead some to a gruff rejection of any initial feeling for the seal: better never to hope and love at all, than to hope and love when some eventual bitter end is a foregone conclusion. Of course, this tragic but understandable reaction is anything but a rejection of the reality of spiritual sensitivity to nonhuman creatures. To the contrary, it speaks to unbearable sensitivity. It betrays unbearable pain. This tragic and spiritually sensitive response calls for spiritual counseling that is beyond the brief of this study. Here the task is to stand in the face of much modern denial and to name and own these spiritual realities in all their complexity.

The worry over the seal, the concern for its desperation, for its survival, the thankfulness for the efforts of the rescue workers, the joy in the seal's release, the joy at its joy, or, perhaps if the orca is what chased it into the shelter of the outtake tank in the first place, the anguish over its anguish, the pain at its despair, the sadness at its death and, from another perspective, the happiness for the orca, for its success in the hunt and in its struggle to survive: all of these spiritual realities in all their complexity and tension *are real*.

I will argue below that these spiritual realities are real in the ordinary and classic moral realist sense. That is, they are not ultimately the products of nature and nurture. They reflect an inherently and irreducibly spiritual dimension of reality. From the perspective of the philosophical spirituality defended here, it is precisely because these spiritual realities are real that

Love Diminished, Love Betrayed

we remain exquisitely sensitive to them despite the incredible alienation mainstream modern Western rationality has so powerfully inscribed into our understanding and against our humanity.

Chapter 2

Morality Diminished, Morality Betrayed

"We are one lesson"

Tragically, the hubristic dimming of our love for all creatures and all creation has helped modern philosophy, science, and theology to diminish and betray profound moral convictions. When the entire world, including all other creatures, is portrayed as a machine, it changes people's moral vision. Instrumentalism becomes basic to ethical understanding vis-à-vis nonhuman creatures and the rest of the world. In an "instrumentalist" vision, value is a function of utility—utility for humans. Once the entire world is rendered machine, that is, with the completion of modernity's hubristic, human-centered revolution, all value is pegged to humans.

For modern ethical instrumentalism, then, "value" equals "value to humans." With regard to anything nonhuman, one can think in terms of toasters. If it's my toaster, I can do whatever I like with it. If it's your toaster, then I should respect it because I should respect you. But the toaster has no value apart from its value to one or more humans. To see all creation as a machine is, ethically, to see all creation as toaster. Then only ethical instrumentalism makes any sense with regard to our ethical responsibilities vis-à-vis nature and nonhuman creatures. Then there is, for instance, no reason to value nonhuman creatures or landscapes that are out there, "not doing anyone any good," for the value of any nonhuman creature or any piece of creation will be pegged to its value for humans.

Few people have ever really believed that all other creatures are wholly biological machines, lacking in any non-derivative value, but instrumentalism continues to wield significant influence. It also tends to align perfectly with human self-interest. In the nineteenth and twentieth centuries, especially in the wake of Darwinism and other advances in biology and brain research, the Cartesian dualism between matter and spirit was rejected. But human hubris endured. Animals were still regarded and treated as machines. As noted, most Christians retained a Gnostic appeal to souls: humans have souls, animals don't. Secular intellectuals looked for Darwinian distinctions: only humans use tools, have cultures, teach their young, create music, create art, use symbols to communicate, have a twenty-five–hour biological clock, have abstract ideas, or are self-aware. All these have been proffered and then refuted as unique distinctions. What's interesting about the refutation of the distinctions is that they have typically been front-page news. Why?

At the turn of the millennium you could read many philosophers' and scientists' condescending responses to Donald Griffin's contentions that animals had minds similar to ours (Griffin, remember, is the scientist who founded the initially ridiculed but increasingly respected and now blossoming field of "cognitive ethology"). One philosopher, Daniel Dennett, voiced the common response that if someone made a robot dog with big eyes that could look happy or sad, that would respond with a smile when you entered a room or look hurt when you yelled, you would react to that robot dog as if it had real feelings. Whether dog or robot, he argued, our reaction is an evolved response to visual cues. To infer from such responses that either the robot or the dog had feelings or a mind would be equally silly.[1] Such ridicule was the standard response of philosophers and scientists until recently. It is still common.

---

1. What Dennett was quoted as saying in his 1995 essay was, "It is in fact ridiculously easy to induce powerful intuitions of not just sentience but full-blown consciousness (ripe with malevolence or curiosity or friendship) by exposing people to quite simple robots made to move in familiar mammalian ways at mammalian speeds" (as quoted by Eakin, "Think Tank"). I am using this illustration to point out the shallowness of a common response. Dennett's fully developed position on animal and human consciousness, with which I would still disagree (and which also rejects, for instance, free will as a human capacity), is considerably more complex (I respond to Dennett in detail in chapter 5).

Part One: Awakening and Agape

In *Kindred Spirits*, veterinarian Allen Schoen talks about working at the Animal Medical Center of the American Humane Society in New York City. Even at the Humane Society medical center as late as 1991, Schoen laments, veterinarians would refer to the animals in their care as "a 1986 model standard poodle," "a 1975 model cocker spaniel," or a "1981 model Great Dane."[2] These were not "Kiki," "Sherlock," and "Sadie," these were biological machines.

As more and more scientists are coming to agree, the common response voiced by Dennett is remarkably weak. Certainly it would be silly to think the robot dog had feelings. But the robot dog and I do not share identical nervous systems, similar brain structure, overwhelming genetic similarity. Given that a real dog is in all these respects very similar to me, there is every reason to conclude that a real dog is experiencing emotions and a sense of communion at least analogous to our own. Thus Dennett's too-quick comparison between real "mammals" (e.g., dogs) and robot mammals (e.g., robot dogs) is not just wrong, it is remarkably weak. This is a very intelligent philosopher offering a very weak argument. What is going on?

Scientists have isolated the biochemical basis of all our feelings and emotions. In various precise circumstances different neurotransmitters are released, flow to receptors, and we feel an emotion. The receptors are not just in our brains, but are scattered throughout our entire bodies. These receptors are not unique to humans, they "exist in all animals," and not only in mammals, they exist even in "one-celled beings."[3]

Brain scans reveal that the activity in different parts of the brain associated with emotions like anger and fear are the same in humans and other animals. Why are we surprised? Given the obvious biological and genetic and behavioral similarities, given evolution, why has the burden of proof been on proving similarity?

Again, what is going on? What is going on when popular culture, scientists, philosophers, and theologians alike strive to seize upon a particular physical trait or mental capacity—use of tools, teaching of young, development of cultures—to distinguish humans from other animals? Why would anyone want to turn a morally trivial distinction into the basis for a

---

2. Schoen, *Kindred Spirits*, 45–47. Encouragingly, Schoen notes that the attitudes among former colleagues at the center had changed considerably and for the better a decade later when he was writing his book.

3. Ibid., 44–45.

wholesale moral exclusion? After all, it is not because humans have trouble distinguishing themselves from other animals. It is not, "at last a distinction! Now I'll know when I'm running into another human." What is at stake here? What is going on?

What these folks are after, I think, is this: they want to draw a line, an absolute moral line. They want to be able to keep saying, "There, I owe to that population no regard, no ethical consideration, no concern whatsoever. I can treat them as I will." Take a real but ethically trivial distinction, and turn it into a basis for wholesale exclusion. Now that is a familiar dynamic: they're not like us, they're not one of us, they're not human, they're not rational, not men, not white ... they have no claim on us, they're animals.

This is the immoral rationalizing Yiddish writer and Nobel Laureate Isaac Bashevis Singer had in mind when he had Herman Gombiner, the hero of his short story, "The Letter Writer," while speaking a eulogy for a mouse, reflect that, "in relation to them, all people are Nazis; for the animals it is an eternal Treblinka."[4]

Jewish German philosopher Theodor Adorno had this in mind when he reputedly said this, "Auschwitz begins wherever someone looks at a slaughterhouse and thinks: They're only animals." Actually, though widely cited, Adorno evidently never said this, but the statement that this poignant quote most likely paraphrases indicates he would have agreed with it. Adorno's actual contention was subtler. It is a reflection upon the significance of the truism that people tend to refer to those they are abusing as animal or subhuman (e.g., as cockroaches, savages). This is what Adorno actually wrote while he was in exile in America during the reign of Hitler:

> The possibility of pogroms is decided the moment when the gaze of a fatally wounded animal falls on a human being. The defiance with which [the human] repels this gaze—'after all, it's only an animal'—reappears irresistibly in cruelties done to human beings, the perpetrators having again and again to reassure themselves that it is 'only an animal,' because they could never fully believe this even of animals.[5]

Christian theologian Sallie McFague cites an account shared by womanist novelist Alice Walker. Walker remembers a horse named Blue who was boarded in a house next door to where she lived. The horse was lonely and bored, "but then," writes Walker:

4. Singer, *Collected Stories*, 750.
5. Adorno, *Minima Moralia*, 105.

Part One: Awakening and Agape

in our second year at the house, something happened in Blue's life. One morning, looking out the window at the fog that lay like a ribbon over the meadow, I saw another horse, a brown one, at the other end of Blue's field. Blue appeared to be afraid of it, and for several days made no attempt to go near. We went away for a week. When we returned, Blue had decided to make friends and the two horses ambled or galloped along together, and Blue did not come nearly as often to the fence underneath the apple tree. When he did, bringing his new friend with him, there was a different look in his eyes. A look of independence, of self-possession, of inalienable horseness. His friend eventually became pregnant. For months and months there was, it seemed to me, a mutual feeling between me and the horses of justice, of peace. I fed apples to them both. The look in Blue's eyes was one of unabashed "this is itness."[6]

When the visiting horse was sent back to its owner, Walker says, Blue became "'like a crazed person,' whinnying and tearing at the ground. Walker remembers Blue's piercing eyes. She says, "If I had been born into slavery and my partner had been sold or killed, my eyes would have looked like that, 'We are one lesson.'"[7]

On this point human hubris often gets the upper hand. I encounter people who are actually indignant over people's concern for nonhuman creatures. They are not only offended but also self-righteous because they are concerned for the poor, or for children—as if love for nonhuman creatures and love for children or the poor were somehow mutually exclusive, as if refraining from participating in the abuse of nonhuman animals or caring for nonhuman animals somehow precludes care and concern for humans, as if it is not *precisely the same spirit of love* that sees the plight of vulnerable people and the plight of other creatures. We are one lesson.

That is why St. Francis of Assisi, who abandoned a life of wealth and privilege, took a vow of poverty, and founded an order dedicated to care for poor and hurting people, also cared for animals so passionately that he became the "patron saint of animals." That is why Albert Schweitzer, who abandoned fame and security as a New Testament professor, studied medicine, and founded a medical mission in Africa, believed that what he called "reverence for life" extended to all creatures, even to the viruses he studied under his microscope. As Albert Schweitzer, Theodor Adorno, St.

---

6. Walker, *Living by the Word*, 6, as cited in McFague, *Super, Natural Christians*, 150.
7. Walker, 7, as cited in McFague, *Super, Natural Christians*, 150.

Morality Diminished, Morality Betrayed

Francis of Assisi, Sallie McFague, Isaac Bashevis Singer, and Alice Walker all realize, we are one lesson.

My favorite love-for-nonhuman-animals movie is the classic *E.T.* E.T. is a loving extraterrestrial who only wants to get back home. E.T. is discovered by a small boy, Eliot, who befriends and hides him. Eventually, government scientists hear the rumors and come to capture E.T. Eliot fears they plan to exploit, even dissect E.T. In the middle of the movie there is a scene in which Eliot is at school in his biology class. He and all his classmates have frogs who are hopping around in jars. They also have chloroform. They are to chloroform the frogs so they can dissect them. The movie flashes between the little boy Eliot and images of E.T. Suddenly, Eliot makes the connection. In a fit of joyous abandon, he leaps up and frees his frog out the window. Moments later all his inspired classmates happily do the same. Everyone in my theater erupted in spontaneous, joyful applause.

These were not animal rights fanatics. But they realized at the core of their beings that there was nothing objective and morally neutral about that science lesson. They realized that the most significant lesson being taught in that scientific lab exercise had little to do with frog anatomy and everything to do with asserting that if people are to be adult, educated, and rational then they should not care about other creatures. That is, it had everything to do with stifling our supposedly childish, romantic, and un-Enlightened love and concern for all creatures: *grow up, be rational, be scientific, stifle your childish emotions, kill the frog.* "NO," said the movie *E.T.*: celebrate the wisdom of the children, not the villains of the movie, the white-coated dissectors, the movie's stand-ins for modern rationality, that moral death that proclaims itself objective enlightenment.[8] There was a reason that people overwhelmingly *loved* the movie *E.T.*, one of the most beloved movies ever produced: their love revealed and implicitly confessed a truth, a truth as objective, as real, and more significant than any strictly scientific conclusion.

What I am trying to do here is to get us to name, consciously and seriously, a spiritual and moral truth that most people already know. Almost everyone is cognizant of nonhuman animals' sensitivities, feelings, and our moral responsibility to treat them lovingly. Despite Descartes, despite

---

8. Notably, in the movie the government scientist leading the effort to capture E.T. is a grown-up version of Eliot and wants only the best for E.T. This portrait of so idealistic a scientist is certainly realistic. Taking it to be representative of the standard or historically predominant institutional or scientific response, however, would be unrealistic and romanticized.

modern science, modern philosophy, and modern theology, despite the powerful denial inscribed in our cultural rhetoric, rationality, and practices, despite the power of human self-interest, *most people already agree about nonhuman animals' sensitivities and feelings, and about our moral responsibility to treat them lovingly.*

Most people, if they saw a four-year-old boy put a firecracker in the mouth of a frog and blow her up would be horrified. They would hope that the boy did not fully understand what he was doing, that he was shocked and disturbed at the result, that he would not harden his heart, that this would be one of those painful memories and lessons he would quietly and repentantly carry with him for the rest of his life.

If he's fifteen and now he's graduated to cats and kerosene, most people are deeply disturbed. If you have any influence, you try to get the child counseling. This child is sick, very possibly wounded himself. People think this not just because they share the common knowledge that kids who torture nonhuman animals regularly become adults who hurt people. They have a sense for the violation of the animal. For the terror, pain, and despair of the cat. And, of course, so does the boy. So does every abuser. The abusers themselves confess their agreement through the abusive behavior itself. It would make no sense to say, "don't hurt that cat, beat up on this toaster instead." The special viciousness and tragic pleasure and self-destructive satisfaction of the abuse turns precisely upon the conviction that the animal feels terror and pain—and if it is one of your own companions (or "pets") who has grown to trust you, even betrayal. At a primordial, emotional level the abuser knows this. *That* is why there is a neat continuity from abuse of other animals to abuse of people.

The real bottom line is this: most people, indeed, *all morally sensitive people* already know that there is a massive spiritual distinction between torching a toaster and torching a cat. Despite widespread denial—even to ourselves—*morally sensitive people already agree.*

If this boy, now a twenty-five-year-old man, moves in next door and still delights in torturing animals? Well, now you should be watching out for the kids, because now you have a disturbed person in the neighborhood. What if another neighbor were to say, "well I don't really care if he tortures cats, they're just cats." Well, frankly, this is bottom-line stuff, and now you should be watching out for that neighbor too. The spiritual truth here is absolutely basic.

Morality Diminished, Morality Betrayed

Of course, there are those who dispassionately and rationally act as if they do not discern this basic spiritual truth—and perhaps they do not. In his subtle and disturbing book, *A Language Older Than Words*, Derrick Jensen reminds us of the experiments of the respected scientists Harry Harlow and Stephen Suomi, which Peter Singer described in his classic, *Animal Liberation*. Harlow and Suomi wondered if they could induce psychopathology in primates by removing baby monkeys from their natural mothers and placing them in cages with "cloth surrogate mothers who could become monsters."[9]

For one experiment, they created a cloth-frame "monster mother" that would "eject high pressure compressed air" and "blow the animal's skin practically off its body." For another experiment, they created a mother "that would rock so violently that the baby's head and teeth would rattle." Finally, they created a "porcupine mother" that on command would "eject sharp brass spikes over all the ventral surfaces of its body."

In the experiment involving the violent rocking mother, the baby monkey simply clung tighter, because, as the scientists reported, "a frightened infant clings tightly to its mother at all costs." In the experiment involving the mother with the ejecting spikes, the baby monkey would wait until the spikes retreated, then return and cling to what it perceived to be its mother.

Harlow and Suomi finally realized that the best monster mothers they could devise were these very baby monkeys, grown to maturity, who themselves had been raised in isolation with fabricated monster mothers. These monkeys were too scared of other monkeys to have sex, so the scientists impregnated them using a device they called a "rape rack." When the babies were born, these mothers had no idea what to do with them. Many of the mothers ignored their infants. Others, in the words of Harlow and Suomi, "were brutal or lethal. One of their favorite tricks was to crush the infant's skull with their teeth." But the "really sickening behavior," they report, "was that of smashing the infant's face to the floor, then rubbing it back and forth."

Such experiments are justified because they involve "only animals," but their results are valid when applied to human psychology only because

---

9. Unless otherwise specified, all quotes in this section are taken from Derrick Jensen, *A Language Older Than Words*, 38–39. Jensen's quotes, which are accurate, are taken from Peter Singer's landmark work, *Animal Liberation*, 31–34. Singer, in turn, is citing a paper by Harlow and Suomi, "Induced Psychopathology in Monkeys," that appeared in *Engineering and Science*. The Harlow and Suomi essay includes, among others, photos of a "monster mother" "smashing her infant's face to the floor" (11).

the monkeys are thought to react emotionally and developmentally like humans. As Harlow and Suomi note, "there is little difference, aside from cultural and cortical factors, between human children and monkey children."[10]

Quite consistently, what Harlow and Suomi say they watched, though without seeing, was not one machine conditioned to break another, but a mother who had been tortured to insanity and raped, crushing her own uncomprehending and despairing infant's skull in her teeth. What for some reason does not seem to occur to them is that—insofar as the monkeys are indeed capable of pain, despair, depression, and anxiety, just like human children, and insofar as all these conditions were caused by experiments that we would not hesitate to condemn as torture if they were conducted upon humans—what for some reason does not seem to occur to them is that their experiments raise a massive ethical issue that at the very least requires explicit acknowledgment and careful consideration.[11]

Many of us were taught about experiments of this sort in school. The question is this: did you spot the monstrous? What sort of spirit can conduct such experiments without a word about the ethical issues or the moral injury? What is wrong with modern science, philosophy, and even theology, that they can foster such a spirit?

In *Animal Gospel*, theologian Andrew Linzey, a preeminent Christian advocate of love for nonhuman animals, describes a tuberculosis experiment: "One test requires the instillation of tuberculin solution in the eye, another the injection of tuberculin into the muscle, and the third a test injection of tuberculin into the skin." There are 160 subjects selected. "The published report describes the discomforts and injuries resulting from the eye test, including 'a decidedly uncomfortable lesion' and 'serious inflammation of the eye.' One observer described the plight of the experimental subjects as follows: '[they] would lie in their beds moaning all night from the pain in their eyes.' Also, 'They kept their little hands pressed over their eyes, unable to sleep from the sensations they had to undergo.'"[12]

---

10. Harlow and Suomi, "Induced Psychopathology in Monkeys," 9.

11. The experiments reported in the "Induced Psychopathology" article had been conducted over the course of around ten years at the University of Wisconsin Primate Laboratories, so may have been reviewed—though no mention of any such review process is made in the article. Investigating that possibility and analyzing the rationale for approving the experiment, if such a rationale was indeed developed, may be illuminating but goes beyond the boundaries of the present reflection.

12. Linzey, *Animal Gospel*, 92–93.

Morality Diminished, Morality Betrayed

Now, "these experiments were performed in 1908 by doctors and associates of the William Pepper Clinical Laboratory of the University of Pennsylvania. The experimental victims, however, were not just any animals but humans—children . . . 160 orphans, all but twenty-six of whom resided in the St. Vincent's Home for Orphans, a Catholic orphanage in Philadelphia."[13]

Linzey goes on to describe the contents of a pamphlet of the New York Anti-Vivisection Society, published in 1915. The pamphlet "details (among other things) the inoculation of consumptive germs, the deliberate injection of syphilis, and the grafting on of malignant cancers." Again, these all name experiments conducted upon humans. Linzey gets this information from Susan E. Lederer's *Subjected to Science: Human Experimentation before the Second World War*. Linzey cites one of Lederer's major findings, "During [the period before the Second World War] the moral issues raised by experimenting on human beings were most intensely pursued by men and women committed to the protection of animals."[14]

It is not the case that love, concern, and respect for other animals competes with love, concern, and respect for humans. To the contrary, it is the same love and concern and respect that one has, *or not*, for all life. We are one lesson. Life, all life, is sacred. The reality here concerns the core of our spirits, the core of our spirituality, the core reality of our moral be-ing. It is not only the well-being of other animals that is at stake here, though obviously those are stakes I am vitally concerned to bring into the light. In an incredibly powerful if unconscious way, we humans ourselves, our spiritual goodness and wholeness and ability to love and respect not only others but our very selves, is vitally at stake.

When one cloaks and betrays one's own profound having been seized by love, that is, when one cloaks and betrays moral reality, one not only harms nonhuman animals, one harms oneself, one afflicts the core of one's spiritual being. The concern here is certainly rooted in love for nonhuman animals, but it is just as certainly rooted in love for humans—even love for those who make themselves enemies of animals, and so do unto animals and themselves monstrous harm. Moreover, the concern here is not only for humans' spiritual well-being, it is also a concern over treatment of humans. A society willing to turn a blind eye to factory farms, a society

---

13. Ibid., 93.
14. Ibid., citing Lederer, *Subjected to Science: Human Experimentation before the Second World War*, xiv–xv.

unwilling to admit that a moral issue is even in play when we experiment upon or kill nonhuman animals for research, food, clothing, or cosmetics, is a society well prepared to turn a blind eye to the exploitation, abuse, and torture of people, even orphans, for we are one lesson.

I hope that experiments like Harlow and Suomi's would now be considered to be beyond the pale (though from what I have read in recent years about laboratory experiments and factory "farms" that is far from certain). In any case, scientists need to publicize and condemn experiments such as those conducted by Harlow and Suomi, as well as those named by Linzey and Lederer. What is needed is frank confession and concern about this awful aspect of the history of modern science, and the cultivation of an awareness of how science can lend itself to justification of such moral horrors.

The situation is parallel to that of Christians vis-à-vis the Crusades, the Inquisition, and the burning of "heretics." We hope that Christians would now consider such practices to be beyond the pale (though from what one hears about some Jew, Muslim, or queer-hating churches, that is far from certain). In any case, Christians should be the first to publicize and condemn this horrifying aspect of their heritage, and to consider carefully how religion can and may still be lending itself to justification of such ethical horrors. Of course, it would be unreasonable to reject Christianity because it has a checkered history. Likewise, it would be unreasonable to reject modern science because of its checkered history. What is needed in both cases is honest confession, and identification of the ways in which religion or science may be vulnerable to appropriation for justification or encouragement of ethically awful practices.

First deer

Let me end this chapter with another tale about people. In the late 1990s, I was at a rural church in a conservative area of Texas giving a special weekend lecture on the Christian call to love creation, including all creatures. After the presentation, as I was fielding questions from some sympathetic listeners, mostly youth, I spotted a gruff-looking, heavy-set older man waiting patiently in the background. He was obviously waiting for a clear field so he could tell me what was on his mind. I remember wearily bracing myself for an angry confrontation. He walked up to me after everyone else had left and his first words only confirmed my fears. He was eager to get

Morality Diminished, Morality Betrayed

started, so he set right in, "I remember when I shot my first deer," he began. "When I got to him," he said, "he was just dying. I could feel his warmth."

He paused, and his voice if anything became even gruffer. "I remember looking down and thinking, 'Now what the hell did I do that for?'"

"I never did it again."

And with that he pulled a long balloon out of his pocket, blew it up, and twisted me a dog-shaped balloon, explaining that in retirement he was volunteering as a clown at the children's hospital down in Austin. "That's what I collect the bears for," he said. Then he turned, walked over to the back corner of the room and hoisted up a large box overflowing with teddy bears. With a wave he walked on out.

I was so stunned I never even said a word to him, though I am sure he must have seen the feeling that had begun to well in my eyes. He had given me an unexpected and profound gift, something he had evidently become adept at doing not only for sick kids.

There is reason for hope. We are afflicted by a love diminished, a love betrayed, and also by a morality diminished, a morality betrayed. But there is reason for hope. For a fiery spark of love burns quietly but fiercely in such human spirits, and at the most unexpected moments they can fill our hearts with the gift of love.

CHAPTER 3

A Spirit Not Quite Lost
Rekindling the Spark

Although I am not remaining within the boundaries of rationality appropriate to modern scientific inquiry or common in modern philosophy, my argument is wholly rational. My argument is also spiritual, that is, it takes into account moral and existential dimensions of existence, dimensions that are methodologically invisible within the natural or human sciences. Working within the domain of the spiritual does not mean entering into the mists of relativistic emotionality or subjective irrationality, nor does invocation of spiritual realities entail rejection of the validity of any of the modern sciences. Spiritual argument rejects only unqualified universalistic claims that do not respect the proper methodological limits of modern scientific inquiry.

I agree that nature and nurture (or, genes and memes) profoundly shape our moral, aesthetic, and spiritual understanding. That fact I do not contest. What is unwarranted and what has essentially become dogma for many modern thinkers is the idea that our moral, aesthetic, and spiritual understanding is *wholly* epiphenomenal (i.e., ultimately derived from brute physical push and pull), *wholly* a product of genetic or sociocultural influences, *wholly* a function of a neo-Darwinian calculus that is *wholly* visible to scientific analysis.

This predominant modern Western philosophical idea has many names, among them "naturalism," "physicalism," "non-reductive physicalism," "materialism," and "scientism" (not to be confused with "science").

A Spirit Not Quite Lost

All of these positions defend the same basic position, which is summed up concisely by a respected philosopher we have already encountered, Daniel Dennett. This quote comes from the beginning of a widely celebrated and lengthy book, *Consciousness Explained*, which attempts to develop a wholly material account of consciousness. Notably, in the book Dennett presumes a philosophical consensus so powerful that he does not even feel a need to defend his materialist starting point. He thinks he only needs to state it:

> ... *materialism*: there is only one sort of stuff, namely *matter*—the physical stuff of physics, chemistry, and physiology—and the mind is somehow nothing but a physical phenomenon. In short, the mind is the brain. According to the materialists, we can (in principle!) account for every mental phenomena using the same physical principles, laws, and raw materials that suffice to explain radioactivity, continental drift, photosynthesis, reproduction, nutrition, and growth. It is one of the main burdens of this book to explain consciousness without ever giving in to the siren song of dualism.[1]

It is not the profound influence of genes or memes or the influence of other material factors that I contest, not at all; I only contest and look to undercut the hegemonic claims of those beguiled by the reductionist *"wholly."* I acknowledge the legitimacy of properly delineated scientific investigation and the powerful role of nature and nurture, but my first and foremost task remains the attempt to make manifest, to articulate, and to reason about the spiritual and moral dimensions of reality.

The reality of love and compassion and care and sorrow is not captured by scientific description. The stories of, for instance, Kiki, the cricket, and the trapped seal and the orca can indeed be described and encountered in part through an exclusively scientific modality. You could measure the degree of sympathetic response in various people, look for correlations between degree of response and likelihood of action, relate those in various instances to the species of animal in question, the socioeconomic status of the observer, and all sorts of other variables. You could then study such incidents in scientific fashion and no doubt develop an ability to predict in a general way the sorts of responses one might expect in relation to an array of different factors and circumstances. All this would be good, valid, and quite likely helpful science.

---

1. Dennett, *Consciousness Explained*, 33.

However, insofar as you look at the event solely in this fashion, solely in and through the spectacles of science, solely in quantitative terms, the existential and moral character of the response, the spiritual reality, will remain in itself invisible. Insofar as you methodologically shut yourself off from moral and spiritual dimensions of reality, you have no ability to name and describe your joy over the many ways in which science is invaluable for securing significant ends for others (e.g., curing diseases, lessening pain, helping life to flourish), for this spiritual dimension of reality is by definition excluded from the empirical vision of science and from the vision of the scientist qua scientist (i.e., of the scientist thinking fully and wholly within the methodological boundaries of science).

Granted, there evidently are people who are not seized spiritually by the joy or pain of other creatures. This seems to be a rare condition and most of us are familiar with it only from movies and television where a psychopath makes the perfect mass murderer (or some such) because they lack any conscience. I am not sure why psychopaths could not be well adjusted in society—perhaps clever enough to make a Hobbesian calculation that dictates civil behavior (though no doubt a story about a well-adjusted psychopath would not garner good television ratings!). At any rate, the evident existence of psychopaths is not a basis for denying the reality of the spiritual realm.

In morally responsive people's reactions to the stories of Kiki, the cricket, the whales, and of the seal and the orca, a spiritual realm becomes undeniably manifest. It is perhaps possible people are all massively self-deceived. Humans may be, in Richard Dawkins's infamous words, "survival machines—robot vehicles blindly programmed to preserve the selfish molecules known as genes."[2] Such an idea is not theoretically impossible. Presently, however, there is no good reason to worry over the truth of what is on its face so absurd a possibility. Indeed, I will argue that at this juncture in the history of human understanding it would be *irrational* to affirm so cynical a conclusion.

At this point, however, I remain focused upon another significant challenge. For modern Western ways of speaking and thinking, even in the humanities, even in theology and ethics, have been decisively shaped by rejection of moral reality. It is critical to develop terminology that represents spiritual realities as precisely as possible. In this chapter, accordingly, I focus upon describing the character of having been seized by love for all

---

2. Dawkins, *The Extended Phenotype*, 14.

Faces, which is to say, in this chapter I focus upon describing the character of agape, which lies at the core of my argument for moral realism. Fortunately, I am preceded in this effort by one of the most original and significant philosophers of the twentieth century, Emmanuel Levinas. Levinas has inspired much of my argument, and I will appropriate key ideas from his philosophy as I attempt accurately to represent spiritual reality.[3]

OF FACES AND FACES

Levinas thinks Western thought stretching back even to the ancient Greeks has systematically alienated us from spiritual dimensions of reality (i.e., he traces the roots and influence of scientism to the ancient Greeks). He argues that predominant streams of Western thought, streams that reached unprecedented levels of influence in modern Western philosophy and science, have deadened our alertness to the Faces of others. As a result, people have fallen asleep (i.e., see *only* an empirical, quantifiable world). This slumber/alienation is momentous because morality (in ways I will detail below) begins *from* the Face of some other. Notably, philosophy that begins from anything like an intentional stance, that is, that begins from individual agency, initiative, or action, as does mainstream modern Western philosophy, theoretically cuts itself off from moral reality. Levinas is desperate to reawaken us to moral reality. More precisely, he is desperate to reawaken us to the Faces of others.

The Face is not the physical or historical face of any other, but that by which people are seized with concern (for the sake of clarity, I am capitalizing "Face" when using it in this special, Levinasian sense). One might feel this most dramatically in moments of crisis. You are the first on scene at an accident and a child is injured and weeping. You watch the news and see stunned and suffering survivors of the tsunami or tornado. In response to those wounded, desperate faces you do not react to an idea that you should help, you do not *decide* to be concerned. You find yourself immediately seized by the Face of the child, by the Faces of all those wounded, suffering, pleading faces. Or perhaps you are walking by a church and you see joyous, laughing newlyweds stepping happily down the steps. Suddenly you are smiling too. You have been seized by the Faces of those newlyweds.

Levinas says that the call of the Face comes whenever one walks down the street and passes another. Those who walk asleep may not hear the call

3. Cf. Greenway, *A Reasonable Belief*, 77–120.

of those Faces. But insofar as one is awake one hears the call of the Face of the other, perhaps a call simply to say "hello." Of course, when walking down a street in Manhattan other quite valid considerations keep one from saying "hello" to every person who walks past. But for those who are awake, it takes effort to ignore even the Faces of strangers. In any case, Levinas wants to awaken us to the spiritual realm of the Other, to the spiritual realm where we find ourselves seized by the Faces of others.

To be seized by the Face of another is to be in proximity to the Face of the other. Proximity in this sense is not a spatial category. One gets a phone call from halfway across the world and suddenly, whether it is joy, grief, or fear, you and the other person are right there beside one another. Spiritually, nothing separates you. You are Face-to-Face. Each of you is seized, grasped, taken up by the Face of the other. On the other hand, you can be talking to someone sitting right next to you and be, spiritually, a world apart. Most people know these moments of the Face-to-Face. They are precious, empowering moments, they bring radical presence, real living, they are timeless but fleeting, and despite their infinite significance, they can be disrupted by the slightest distraction. A car cuts us off in traffic, and we return to our walking slumber.

To the degree you are seized by the Face of any other, to that degree that other initiates a moral claim upon you. That is, to be seized by the Face is to know the moral claim and to know the moral claim is to be seized by the Face. There is no deduction here. This is not a circular argument because in the textbook, deductive sense this is not an argument at all. Nor, given the primordial character of having been seized by the Face of another, is any argument from any more primordial basis possible. That is, there is not and could not possibly be an argument from any more fundamental premises because we are describing and naming the sheerest lived immediacy. There is no more primordial "given" (e.g., no sensation, no idea) that could provide more certain epistemological foundations from which a moral argument could be constructed.

The circularity of "to be seized by the Face is to know the moral claim and to know the moral claim is to be seized by the Face," is deliberate and meaningful, for to garner the meaning of the statement you have to free yourself from the play of signs. The tautology pushes you beyond the boundaries of language to the reality spurring us to signify. The description has spiritual force not because of the strength of its inferential structure, but because you are seized by its truth. Frankly, you are either seized by the reality I am gesturing towards here or you are not. You are either seized by love for Faces or you are not. You either recognize the offense of torching the cat or you are profoundly cut off from moral reality. You have either been seized by the sheer immediacy and glory of Face-to-Face encounter or you are alienated from what is most profound, precious, and glorious in life.

As a result of the anthropocentrism (i.e., human-centeredness) of modern Western rationality, Levinas himself remains profoundly alienated from a plenitude of glorious Faces (in his theory, at any rate), for he formally restricts his ascription of "Face" only to humans. But when one gains a sense of what Levinas is talking about with his "Face" language, and when one realizes that being seized by the Face of another is not primordially a conceptual/linguistic event, but a direct and more primordial encounter, a spiritual encounter, the sort of encounter that lies before and beneath all moral language, one quickly understands why Levinas's anthropocentrism wrongly denies human sensitivity to a host of nonhuman Faces. Let me attempt to make all of this clear in the modality of the humanities by means of a thought experiment.

Seeing all Faces

Imagine I walk outside and return with a stick that has fallen to the ground. I hand you the stick. I ask you to break it into pieces. You may give me an odd look, but unless you're a particularly disagreeable person, I imagine you'd break the stick to humor me, no problem. Take a moment to visualize that.

Now imagine that I hand you a small cat (*do not* visualize this). The cat is bound so he cannot resist or hurt you. And now I make the same request. I ask you to break the cat, for instance, to break one of his legs. Assuming that you are not evil or somehow psychopathic (i.e., you are not suffering from a brain injury or are for some other reason unable to be seized by love for Faces—and here let us be sure to remind ourselves of the Faces of psychopaths), I fully expect that you would not be willing to humor me, though I will briefly digress to mention one non-psychopathic exception.

Perhaps someone decides they want to make a point, to assert their superiority and pride of place as human. So they determine that they will defeat their moral impulses, brace themselves, self-overcome their own most primordial, moral self, having been seized, and break the leg of the cat. This is possible, but the effort required in order to squelch one's own clear concious having been seized reveals that it is not a counterexample. To the contrary, the need to brace and self-overcome in and of itself reveals that one is fully alive to the Face of the cat. It also testifies to the perverse willfulness of one's violation of one's own having been seized. One is, after all, not bracing oneself against anyone else's opinions, one is bracing oneself against the condemnation and revulsion of *one's own* having been seized.

Let us assume that you are neither self-defeatingly, willfully evil, nor are you psychopathic, and so you are not willing to humor me when I ask you to break the leg of the cat. I am not evil enough to ask you to visualize yourself breaking the cat's leg, for seriously visualizing oneself doing such a thing would be to inflict violence upon one's self. Why? Why our sense that even visualizing such a thing would be harmful? Why is there violation? Precisely because of the reality of the profound having been seized so many modern critics and even many ethicists confusedly or manipulatively demand we *set aside* in the name of objectivity in order to have a rational moral discussion. That is, precisely because you find yourself seized by the Face of the cat. You have been seized by the sacredness of the life of the cat. This is the moral reality that modern theory suppresses, but by which we thoroughly modern twenty-first-century Westerners are nonetheless still so powerfully seized.

It is worth pausing here and meeting another common objection to this whole way of affirming spiritual realities by specifying why I use the phrase "having been seized," where one might expect to see "intuit" or even "sense." The reason, as the reference to "sense," immediately suggests, is my desire to avoid a term that immediately invokes a fundamentally intentional self and an empirical, subject-object split. Both "intuit" and even more obviously "sense" suggest that there is something out there to be discerned, that you sense a Face "out there," and that all the spiritual energy in the dynamic flows from some "I" that is observing, intuiting, thinking, deciding, or intending. Along this trajectory even self-knowledge is a result of an internalized subject-object split. One "introspects," "looks inward," as if one is observing in oneself an outside of the inside.

To speak of sensing or intuiting something fails to articulate accurately the immediate, pre-intentional, initially passive, profoundly powerful dynamic of having been seized by love for a Face. In this sense our having been seized is more primordial than knowledge or intentionality. Though typically we are almost instantly reflectively aware of our having been seized, this is after the fact awareness. The spiritual truth of the having been seized, agape, is not a result of introspection (with its lurking infinite regress) or ascription (i.e., considered judgment). Spiritual truths seize us primordially and are reflected upon after the fact. "Agape" and "having been seized by love for all Faces" are after the fact significations of a more primordial reality.

In all these ways the moral vocabulary of "responsibility" is astoundingly precise and revealing (if still too wooden and abstract to capture the glory or pathos by which we are seized). There is nothing out there in the cat that we directly observe that is the Face of the cat. There is not some combination of sense impressions that combine to constitute the Face of the cat. Rather, *in response* to the proposed abuse of the cat the Face of the cat is manifest. The Face is mediated physically, through the senses, but it is not itself physical in the modern sense of "matter," "energy," "wave," or "extension." We realize we have been seized by the Face of the cat in our response, in our "having been seized." In our having been seized, the Face of the cat and our own responsibility are immediately manifest. Accordingly the first and foremost question that confronts us is not scientific or epistemological (i.e., philosophical in the modern Western sense). The first and foremost question is spiritual and moral: will we deny and resist or acknowledge and act in response to our having been seized?

Let me take this thought experiment a step further. Imagine not a stick and not a cat, but a young tree, perhaps a maple sapling. I take you over to the sapling, which is in a splendid location, not in the way of anything, and I say, "rip it out of the ground so it cannot possibly recover." My hunch is that few people would do this to humor me. The sense of violation is not nearly so great as in the case of the cat, but nonetheless there is a sense of violation, and one would need more of a reason than simply to humor me to destroy that sapling. One has been seized by the Face of the sapling.

I can imagine someone grabbing that sapling with vindictiveness and destroying it because they are eager to seize the opportunity to prove us wrong, to assert themselves over and against the call of that Face. I can even imagine them taking a perverse pleasure in their assertion of will over and against their own having been seized. Most likely it will be easier for them to overcome their own having been seized in this case with the sapling than it was in the case of the cat. But the perverse spiritual energy flowing through such an encounter does nothing to disprove the reality and call of the Face. To the contrary, the sense of it as a powerful act stems precisely from the strength of the exertion—not the physical exertion of pulling out the sapling, but the spiritual exertion of defeating and violating one's own profound having been seized by the sacredness of the life of the sapling, that is, the spiritual exertion of violating one's own having been seized by the Face of the sapling.

For most people, the sense for the moral violation involved in killing the sapling is not equivalent to the sense of violation with regard to the breaking of the cat, let alone with regard to the breaking of a human (where the sense of violation is so strong that I refrained from even setting up the scenario—for consistency I should have added a little boy to the list of stick, sapling, cat, but I could not bring myself to do so except in this oblique manner).

What I hope to make evident is the reality of our primordial having been seized by love for a Face whenever any life, even the life of a sapling, is destroyed. I have also suggested that there is a gradation in our valuing. That is, there is typically a difference in the degree of our sense of violation vis-à-vis the stick, the sapling, the cat, and the little boy. The issues surrounding this ethical gradation among Faces are complex, and I will address them in detail below. In broad terms, I will conclude that anyone who would as soon kill the boy as kill the sapling, or who would as soon break the cat as kill the sapling, is profoundly lacking in ethical judgment.

Given the predominance of human hard-heartedness, it is important to stress that even if one's sense for the evil of breaking the sapling is far less potent than one's sense for the breaking of the cat (let alone the boy), spiritual giants will be mortified over wanton destruction even of the sapling, and they will be saddened even if its destruction was deemed prudent (e.g., because it is necessary for fuel or shelter for the boy). Unfortunately, given the ways in which modernity has blunted moral consciousness, the moral sensitivity of most modern Westerners is dulled once one moves beyond consideration of humans. It takes heightened moral sensitivity to remain awake amidst the rush and stresses of daily life to the profound moral worth of a sapling.

Notably, since moral sensitivity even to a sapling is the same moral sensitivity one should have for humans, those with extreme sensitivity to saplings should simultaneously be those who are most profoundly sensitive to the needs of other humans (else there is serious ethical confusion).[4]

---

4. Sometimes one hears, as an utterly bizarre objection to concern for all creatures, even saplings, that "Hitler loved his dogs." Hitler was, to say the very least, ethically

A Spirit Not Quite Lost

Moral sensitivity should broaden out and include an ever richer and more diverse array of living beings as it becomes more refined. It is not "either plants or humans," or "either humans or other animals." It is the same spirituality that loves the boy, the cat, and the sapling. One who is supremely sensitive even to the violation involved in the destruction of the life of a plant should be exquisitely sensitive to the violation involved in the destruction of human life, for we are one lesson. All life is sacred. It is one and the same love, one and the same spirituality that we affirm and foster or that we squelch and destroy.

Unfortunately, in modern Western society "tree hugger" has not typically named the exquisitely sensitive soul, has not named the exemplary moral sensitivity and love of the saint. Instead of being a phrase of admiration, a naming of those whose spiritual sensitivity is so refined they feel compelled to sacrifice life energy for the sake of saving trees, "tree hugger" is in many influential circles a phrase of derision. This is a stark sign of an alienation from life that permeates Western society.

Distinguishing "Morality" from "Ethics"

Levinas often described himself as doing "the ethics of ethics." Levinas is left with this literally nonsensical phrase because he remains bound by the limits of precisely the modern vocabularies he is critiquing. I want to demarcate a helpful distinction between morality and ethics. Namely, I will use "moral" to gesture toward agape, toward the reality of having been seized by love, so that we are repulsed by horrible events and moved by wonderful events. On the other hand, I will use "ethical" to refer to how having been seized is best articulated in terms of principles, and to name the reasoning utilized to move from primordial having been seized to what are often complex ethical rationales and judgments.

---

confused, and the inconsistency of his purported "love" is an indication of his ethical confusion/perversity of spirit (and in his horrible case, this is the least of the indicators). Obviously, it is not always or even usually the case that people who love dogs hate other people. Where this is the case, it is not a counterexample, but an obvious manifestation of ethical confusion. At bit more realistically, I do sometimes meet people who seem to dislike people but love other animals. In some cases, there are intense, tragic personal histories that explain this discrepancy, and such cases call for careful and sympathetic response. In other cases, forms of ethical confusion far more mild than Hitler's but nonetheless problematic may be in play and should be addressed.

PART ONE: AWAKENING AND AGAPE

In these terms, my argument aims to awaken and legitimate *moral* reality; that is, my argument aims to aid us in naming and consciously opening ourselves to having been seized by love for Faces, the having been seized which reveals the sacredness of all life. Even after we are *morally* awakened, the complexities of real life and individual fallibility require careful *ethical* reflection and debate as we try to determine how best to realize our moral ideals in a conflicted world.

On this understanding, most of what has been called either "ethics" or "morality" in the modern period falls under the category of "ethics." The category of the "moral" in my classic sense, by contrast, has been almost wholly elided by modern Western rationality. But, again, what is meant here by "moral" is not unfamiliar. Morality names primordial having been seized by love for Faces, the passion that fires commitment to goodness, justice, and the struggle against injustice and evil. This reflects the popular and classic understanding of what at heart morality has always been understood to be, a real part of the ultimate fabric of reality.

One might say that ethics without morality is empty, and that morality without ethics is formless and void. A bit less neatly but more precisely, one might say that ethics without morality is empty, and that morality without ethics lacks conceptual form, intersubjective refinement and confirmation, and the ability to address carefully the complexities of ethical quandary cases (e.g., wherein we have been seized by love for diverse Faces whose respective needs are in tension, or where what would be best is not clear). We need both morality and ethics. Morality comes first, for ethics without morality is empty. What Levinas calls "the ethics of ethics" I would call "the morality of ethics." There is definitely a need for reasoned ethical debate in the ordinary modern sense, but only in the ongoing wake of one's primordial having been seized by love for every Face (that is, only in the wake of moral reality) are ethical arguments not empty.

Finally, and in a slightly different vein, in terms of this morality/ethics distinction one might say that while any animal (including humans) can only do ethics in proportion to linguistic/cognitive capacity, and thus ethics is possible for animals only insofar as they have advanced linguistic capacity, moral capacity requires only the ability to be seized by love for the Face of another, and such genuine moral capacity may be shared by numerous creatures with limited or no linguistic capacities (from multiple species). Moreover, there is every reason to think that self-awareness, degrees of agency, and the ability to form affective bonds is shared by even

A Spirit Not Quite Lost

more animals (i.e., including some not capable of ethics or morality). Furthermore, it is reasonable to suppose that a capacity to enjoy and to suffer is shared in some rudimentary way even by the most primitive life forms (remember those "emotion" chemicals released even by one-celled organisms).[5]

Accordingly, while it is reasonable to conclude that only advanced, language-capable creatures are capable of ethical reflection, and while it is reasonable to expect only more cognitively advanced (though not necessarily concept-capable) creatures to be moral (i.e., to be seized by the Faces of others), this does nothing to invalidate or truncate the parameters of cognitively advanced creatures' moral response ability and responsibility, it does nothing to invalidate cognitively advanced creatures' having been seized by love for and ethical responsibility to the Faces of *all* creatures—even of that sapling, which is certainly not capable of ethics and that almost certainly is not moral, but which in a rudimentary but nonetheless real, living fashion enjoys flourishing.

Notably, some such gradation of capacities is just what anyone with an evolutionary understanding of the development of life should expect. This brief, programmatic note on the ethical/moral potentials of diverse creatures remains rough, but it provides sufficient general orientation to the issue. Further investigation into the degree to which various creatures or species possess various capacities is not a philosophical question but a scientific one, and so falls beyond the purview of this study.

An Enchanted World

I was walking along Plaza Square in Santa Fe, New Mexico on a clear summer day when I saw a big brown dog lying on the sidewalk. It looked to be a pretty ordinary mutt. What made it extraordinary was the cat that was asleep on its back. That made the cat extraordinary enough, but what made the cat even more extraordinary was the white mouse asleep between her paws and on the dog's back. I had been stopped short by this sight and had really just begun to take it in when suddenly a man's hand reached out from behind a doorway and gave the dog a friendly scratch on the head. The man

---

5. I am here broaching questions about capacity that demand scientific analysis. I am not concerned to survey the results of pertinent scientific explanation here, but only to help remove conceptual blinders that keep many scientists from even conceiving of these as real questions, and to encourage this growing frontier of scientific research.

was evidently the companion of the animals, and at this signal the dog, with the cat and mouse on its back—and now all were awake—got up and started walking with the man down the street in front of me. You should have seen all the smiles that greeted that sight. People happily snapped pictures. Excited children jumped, pointed, and grinned. A circle of happiness radiated out from that blessed vision of a peaceable world.

Is the picture unrealistic? In a certain ecological sense it is undoubtedly unrealistic. But equally unrealistic are dreams of a world free of war, free of horrific disease, free of injustice and cruelty. That certainly does not make such dreams wrong, let alone serve as a basis for rejecting struggles against war, disease, injustice, and cruelty. It just means we should remember to be realistic. For instance, we should acknowledge that we will never live in a world free of predation. There will always be nonhuman animals preying on animals and people, and there will always be people preying on animals (including other people), from murderers, pedophiles, cheats, and robber barons in fancy suits to trophy hunters and factory "farmers."

Even those who strive to live doing as little harm to any creature as possible are caught within a world in which to live is inevitably, to some degree, to destroy. Realism about the moral ills that will continue into the conceivable future is certainly no rejoinder to naming and resisting the evils, no matter if our efforts can never ultimately be made permanent or complete. We are called to the struggle whether or not success is ensured or even possible. Our inability to be perfect is no excuse for not being as good and loving as possible, no excuse for not walking on earth as lovingly as possible.

A couple of years later while changing television channels I happened upon video of that same dog, cat, and mouse. But this time the context was one of those reality shows that delights in viewing vicious animal attacks or accidents in extreme sports competition. The video stayed close in on the dog, cat, and mouse. In this video you didn't get to see the smiles of the children and other passers-by. In the voice-over a macho narrator proclaimed his offense at this violation of the natural order. In his world the strong attack the weak and eat them. He made repeated references to "burgers." Animals are there for the eating. He proclaimed himself *offended* by this vision of friendship and peace among animals (his more sophisticated sympathizers might make condescending references to an unrealistic romanticizing of nature).

A Spirit Not Quite Lost

His response is tragic and dangerous to peace on earth—in this sense his response was evil. In the real world one will never fully overcome such violent and spiteful responses. Nonetheless, one is moved by having been seized by love for the Faces of all others to struggle for the good, to struggle to maximize the smiles and the delight.

Just after the turn of the millennium, a pastor from Zambia was selected by his denomination to pursue a year of theological study abroad, and he studied all of these ideas in a class of mine, "Nature, Theology, and Ethics." Modern Western intellectual trajectories that alienate us from creation have had a significant impact in much of Africa, especially among Christians. This Zambian pastor found the class material very applicable, and was even able to reconnect to some traditional African ways of valuing creation that he had mistakenly thought to be invalidated by Christian belief (the culprit was really modern Western rationality).

Toward the end of the semester he shared two stories with the class to illustrate his spiritual reawakening. "The other day I was about to turn on the shower in the dorm," he said, "when I looked down and saw an ant by the drain. Before I would have just turned the shower on and washed that ant down the drain. But this time I stopped, got the ant on a piece of paper, put my bathrobe on, went outside, and let it go on the grass."

On another day he was walking through the park when he saw a dead bird under a bush. "Before," he said, "I would have walked by that bird without pausing. But this time I knelt down by the bird, I stayed there quietly for a few moments and thought of its life and death, and I said a prayer for that bird before I moved on."

To *attend*, to consciously take the time to open our spiritual sensitivities even to ants and birds, not only on special occasions but amidst the ordinary run of our daily lives, is a form of spiritual discipline, a spiritual discipline that enlivens and re-enchants a confusedly disenchanted world, a spiritual discipline that brings intense joy and delight as well as sadness and pain. The modern disenchantment of the world was neither enlightened nor enlightening. Philosophy's hubristic and hegemonic extension of the explanatory, experimental, and logical techniques of modern science into every domain of reflection elided the Faces of all nonhuman creatures.

In particular, the modern fantasy of a disenchanted world advanced the philosophical claim that the only reality that ultimately existed was the reality that scientific reflection could see and adjudicate. This was a claim that removed all external authority—indeed, all having been seized—until

Part One: Awakening and Agape

only the individual human mind or soul was not reduced to a thing amidst the flow. Of course, though still not popularly recognized, in time the logic of this dialectic of disenchantment inexorably extended its reach without qualification to the human, until the final ghost of what was once signified by "mind," "soul," "spirit," or "Face" was exorcised from the machine.

Even after the systemic distortion afflicting modern Western rationality is unveiled it remains potent. I would not be surprised if many readers, despite their resonance with my moral stories and their shared concern over Kiki, the cricket, the whales, the seal, Alice Walker's horses, and those poor orphans, hesitate nonetheless over the reasonableness of understanding all of this as an awakening to primordial moral reality. The power of the philosophical premise that undergirds the systemic distortion, a premise known as materialism, physicalism, naturalism, metaphysical naturalism, or scientism (not to be confused with science), the power of that philosophical premise is immense.

Enduring suspicion at this point would be warranted, for I have not yet directly discredited scientistic premises, though by now I hope that the reality of scientism's devastating denial of moral reality is clear. At any rate, in the next chapter I criticize scientism directly. I will not here be able to prove that scientism is false, but I will be able to establish that, given the current state of human understanding, it is irrational to affirm that scientism is true.[6] If that is the case, then at present it is wholly reasonable to contend that our moral and spiritual awakening unveils primordial truth about the ultimate character of reality, and it is wholly reasonable to contend that we suffer from a love diminished, a love betrayed.

---

6. In Greenway, *A Reasonable Belief*, 77–100, I develop a more aggressive argument for the incoherence of scientism.

Part Two

SCIENCE, SCIENTISM, MORALITY

Chapter 4

Science not Scientism

A predominant mainstream modern Western philosophical understanding that rejects the reality of agape is variously called materialism, naturalism, metaphysical naturalism, physicalism, non-reductive physicalism or, as I will call it, scientism. It is critical that I take scientism on explicitly because while those who accept modernity's predominant, scientistic understanding of the ultimate character of reality will almost certainly acknowledge the emotional power of my argument, they will reject the possibility that we have been awakened to anything more than an evolved emotional response. Since I accept evolutionary theory, I agree that the dynamics of awakening include evolved emotional response. I will argue, however, that there is no reason to think that awakening is *only* an evolved emotional response. To the contrary, it is reasonable to think we are awakened to moral reality. Those committed to scientism reject that possibility, and nothing I have said so far would compel them to acknowledge that they are unwarranted in rejecting moral realism. Making clear that affirmation of scientism is presently unwarranted, and making clear how we can affirm both science (not scientism) and moral reality is the prime task of part two of my argument, "Science, Scientism, Morality."

Defenders of scientism often attempt to protect their position by identifying scientism with modern science and accusing critics of scientism of rejecting science. Let me immediately stress that I do not debate the specific scientific conclusions of astronomy, biology, chemistry, physics, psychology, sociology, or any other science. In particular, my position does not require anyone to reject evolutionary biology, the unimaginably vast age and size of the cosmos, or even the quite real possibility of life on other planets.

The problem comes only when one denies that there is any reality beyond the sphere of the natural, for such denial shifts us from science to scientism. This is significant because, as will become clear, when one denies that there is any reality beyond the natural sphere then one eliminates, as classically and ordinarily understood, free will, creative originality, moral reality, moral responsibility, and the possibility of any divine reality. This is problematic not simply because these are capacities and realities fundamental to human self-understanding and culture, but because at present there is no good reason to conclude that scientism is true. Again, as will become clear, to reject scientism is not to reject science. Scientism itself is not a scientific conclusion. It is a philosophical contention. It is not *necessarily* untrue. But at present there is no good reason to conclude that it is true.

Scientism by default

Let me begin by explaining scientism using some very familiar categories. Most of us will remember the great nature/nurture debate from high school. The question is, "to what degree is our behavior determined by nature and to what degree is our behavior determined by nurture?" The debate is typically resolved amicably enough with the conclusion that it is almost always some combination of the two, and one is left to quibble over how precisely to apportion the influence of nature and/or nurture with regard to particular cases.[1]

The nature/nurture and/or, however, is not innocent. There is no problem with the two key questions, "To what degree nurture?" and "To what degree nature?" Certainly my actions are to a significant degree determined by nature. And certainly my actions are to a significant degree determined by nurture. That is, all of my actions are indeed significantly determined by nature and/or nurture. But that legitimate conclusion is betrayed when one frames the nature/nurture debate without qualification, and so *by default poses within an exhaustive and/or framework* the question: "to what degree is my behavior determined by nature and/or to what degree is my behavior determined by nurture?" When this and/or framework is presented without

---

1. I use this nature/nurture illustration and unfold and respond to its implications in far more detail in Greenway, *A Reasonable Belief*, 3-54.

qualification it surreptitiously shifts us from science to scientism. For when the framework is posed without qualification, then the question is framed in such a way that answers can appeal only to the influence of nature and/or nurture, perhaps leaving some space for indeterminacy/randomness. That is, the explanatory options are limited to nature *and/or* nurture. In other words, "to what degree nature and to what degree nurture?" is then framed such that one will answer "30/70 nature/nurture," or "40/60 nature/nurture," or "50/50," or perhaps "49/50 nature/nurture with 1 percent indexed to sheer randomness."

The implications of this exhaustive and/or framework are straightforward and anything but obviously true or innocent. The exclusive and/or means, for instance, that when one asks about the sources of one's actions there is no possibility of asking, "to what degree free will?" or "to what degree creative originality?" or "to what degree a response to moral reality?" or "to what degree a response to the call of the divine?" That is, built into the nature/nurture and/or as commonly taught without qualification is a rejection of free will, a rejection of creative originality, a rejection of moral action and of moral responsibility in the ordinary sense, and a rejection of the possibility of any divine influence upon humans or upon any earthly realities, for my every movement, every thought, and every decision is wholly determined, aside from the possibility of some utter randomness, by causal streams of nature/nurture conditioning that precede my birth and flow on beyond my death.

With the standard, unqualified nature/nurture and/or framing, then, we are shifted from the non-debatable claim that to a significant degree my behavior is determined by nature and to a significant degree my behavior is determined by nurture to the highly debatable claim that all of my behavior is *wholly* determined by some combination of nature and/or nurture, save perhaps leaving some minimal role for randomness. In this way, without explicit mention, let alone any actual argument, we are shifted from science to scientism. That is, we are shifted surreptitiously and illicitly from science, taken as an accurate but partial reflection of reality, to scientism, which takes modern scientific vision to possess, in principle, an exhaustive view of reality. We are moved to a position that has no space for saying, for instance, that my action was "54 percent nature, 40 percent nurture, 1 percent random, and 5 percent (a critical, tilt-the-balance degree) free agency and/or response to moral reality."

PART TWO: SCIENCE, SCIENTISM, MORALITY

We are so accustomed to thinking of the nature/nurture debate as exhausting the explanatory options that my suggestion that we accord something like 5 percent to free agency or moral responsiveness can look very odd, but in fact my proposal accurately reflects ordinary understanding. For instance, when in a court of law we consider not guilt or innocence but what sentence to impose upon the guilty, we quite reasonably consider it proper to take into account nature (e.g., to what degree was the violence largely the result of the pressures a tumor was putting onto a part of the brain?), nurture (e.g., to what degree was the violence largely a result of sustained and horrific abuse that the convicted party endured from his or her own parents?), as well as free agency (e.g., to what degree is there no excuse for the behavior, to what degree is the defendant morally culpable). Free agency and agape by definition cannot be seen by science and my delineation of precise percentages is fanciful, but the point is nonetheless clear: unless there is compelling reason to do so, we should not make the shift from science to scientism. I will argue that there is no compelling reason to affirm scientism.

An understandable temptation

It is easy to understand why first-rate scientists are tempted to go beyond science and affirm scientism. The goal of any particular scientific investigation is to provide a complete explanation for a given effect. It may be helpful to distinguish roughly between *necessary* and *sufficient* causes or conditions and also between *correlations* and *causal connections*. A necessary condition is one that is necessary to a given effect. For instance, oxygen is necessary if one is going to have fire. But a necessary condition is not enough to result in an effect. One can have oxygen without fire. Sufficient conditions are that set of conditions that necessarily result in the effect. Paper, oxygen, and a temperature of 800 degrees constitute sufficient conditions for fire. That is, if one has paper, oxygen, and a temperature of 800 degrees, one will have fire. The goal of scientific explanation is to delineate *sufficient* conditions for a given effect. That is, to identify conditions sufficient to produce that effect.

One could realize that paper, oxygen, and a temperature of 800 degrees always gives you fire without having scientific understanding of the event. That is, one could simply be aware of the consistent correlation among these conditions and fire. To have scientific knowledge, one would also

Science not Scientism

need to be able to delineate how the mechanisms work. One would need to be able to detail the causal relationships among paper, oxygen, and a temperature of 800 degrees that result in fire. A complete scientific explanation, in short, would involve both the ability to delineate sufficient conditions for any effect and the ability to explain the causal mechanisms leading from the causes to the effect. Typically, once the sufficient conditions and all the causal connections have been delineated, an explanation of the relationship between causes and effects is considered complete or proven. Shy of such explanatory completeness, one can still use the ideal of such a complete explanation as a measure against which to judge various explanations (i.e., which fall closer to or further from the ideal of being "proven").

My goal here is not to give a detailed account of scientific method or standards for scientific proof, but to consider a powerful effect of the modern explanatory ideal, which is now clear enough for present purposes. For obvious reasons, the drive to provide complete explanations, the drive to delineate, without remainder, all the causal links, to delineate sufficient conditions, to develop a complete explanation, the drive to push the boundaries of scientific knowledge ahead as far as possible and to push indeterminacy and the unknown as far back as possible, such a drive to complete explanation will be "in the DNA," so to speak, of first-rate scientists.

This drive to push scientific explanation forward as far as possible should be encouraged. This drive for complete explanation, however, can provide ample impetus for the shift from legitimate affirmation of science to illegitimate affirmation of scientism. One expects scientists as scientists to feel compelled to search tirelessly for scientific explanations, to push the boundaries of science to the utmost limit. This is an admirable trait in a scientist. Its shadow side, however, is a tendency to facilitate an illicit shift from science to scientism, to tempt scientists to assert that in principle science has no limits, that every effect (including all human thought and action) is wholly the product of antecedent causal streams (possibly in combination with some degree of randomness/indeterminacy). This tendency is further facilitated by the fact that the shift from science to scientism has been inscribed into modern rationality with such subtlety that its reality and stakes are invisible with regard to something so common and seemingly innocent as the framing of the nature/nurture and/or (which, with its denial of free will, moral action, moral responsibility in the ordinary sense, and any possible divine influence, is not at all innocent).

Part Two: Science, Scientism, Morality

Accordingly, for mainstream late twentieth century secular understanding, every subject (i.e., every "I") is a narrative fiction designating a significant locus from the perspective of one level of understanding/interpretation (e.g., the human), but what is thus designated "subject" is ultimately part of the flow of a mindless (i.e., largely deterministic, possibly partly random) flux. This is the perspective Richard Dawkins reflects in *The Selfish Gene* with his notorious contention that the decisive evolutionary unit is not any individual creature but the replicators that use groups of creatures to replicate themselves. These replicators

> swarm in huge colonies, safe inside gigantic lumbering robots, sealed off from the outside world, communicating with it by tortuous indirect routes, manipulating it by remote control. They are in you and in me; they created us, body and mind; and their preservation is the ultimate rationale for our existence. They have come a long way, these replicators. Now they go by the name of genes, and we are their survival machines.[2]

Note that the "selfish" in Dawkins's title is not ethical in the classic sense. It only describes certain blind tendencies that describe characteristic behavior of some survival machines as they "beat out" others in a "struggle" for existence. The same holds for the different blind tendencies described by Mark Ridley in *The Cooperative Gene*.[3] Genes are not selfish or cooperative. They are mindless parts of the physical flow.

The case of the missing argument

Significantly, no argument has established that reality is confined within the bounds of what is directly or indirectly visible to science. That is, no argument has established that there is no reality beyond the physical sphere. No one has established that the realities seventeenth-century philosopher Rene Descartes famously ascribed to the realm of "spirit"—for instance, the reality of free and morally responsible agents—no argument has established

---

2. Dawkins, *The Selfish Gene*, 19–20. Dawkins did not seem fully to grasp the philosophical implications of his position for realities such as human free will and moral responsibility.

3. Ridley, *The Cooperative Gene*. For the sake of clarity and precision, biologists should avoid using terms like "selfish" and "cooperative," which carry intentional/agentival and moral connotations with no legitimate place within the parameters of the modern science of biology, and instead use terms such as "parasitic" and "symbiotic."

that such realities do not exist. Rather, the undeniable success of the sciences has led many (but far from all) philosophers, and many (but far from all) scientists speaking as philosophers to such enthusiasm over the reach of scientific reasoning that it has fueled the contention that there simply is no reality beyond that which is visible through the empirical spectacles of modern science.

Notably, there is nothing new about this powerful drive to push beyond science to scientism. And there is nothing new about premature proclamations of the truth of scientism. As far back as 1814, Pierre-Simon Laplace famously contended that:

> An intellect which at any given moment knew all the forces that animate Nature and the mutual positions of the beings that comprise it, if this intellect were vast enough to submit its data to analysis, could condense into a single formula the movement of the greatest bodies of the universe and that of the lightest atom: for such an intellect nothing could be uncertain; and the future just like the past would be present before its eyes.[4]

Laplace here presumes that the ideas of causation and necessary connection inferred from study of objects such as planets are accurate not only in relation to those objects, but also exhaustively. That is, Laplace leaps from limited evidence to global conclusions, taking laws derived from analysis of the motion of planets and presuming that they would also apply without remainder to humans. Given the limitations of contemporary physics, let alone biology and chemistry (which had barely emerged as sciences in 1814), it is remarkable that Laplace's claim did not emerge as a textbook example of hasty generalization (i.e., leaping too quickly from limited knowledge to expansive knowledge claims). Amazingly, many advocates of scientism hail Laplace's famous contention as smart and prophetic.

Laplace was, to say the least, radically premature. His conclusion would still be unwarranted. Indeed, far from Laplace's contention being confirmed over the course of the intervening two centuries, by the late twentieth century it had become common to hear scientists quip that the universe may be not only stranger than we have imagined, but stranger than we *can* imagine. So we can say that while scientism is *perhaps* possible, there is presently no good reason to think that it is true. To be sure, this is not to reject science. It is to be clear about both the incredible power of

---

4. Laplace, *A Philosophical Essay on Probabilities*, as cited in Dennett, *Freedom Evolves*, 28.

modern science and also about the limits of modern science. Insofar as we do choose freely, insofar as we do act and write and draw creatively, insofar as we are seized by love for the Faces of others, the bounds of scientific inquiry and explanation are limited. Scientific explanations are significant but incomplete when these extraphysical realities are in play.

According to partisans of scientism, aside from the possibility of sheer randomness in reality, there is in principle no limit to the bounds of scientific explanation. *If* the bounds of scientific exploration and explanation are indeed coterminous with the bounds of reality and are in principle unlimited (or, with regard to explanatory potential, are limited in principle only by true randomness/indeterminacy within reality), then one must deny, in the classic moral realist or idealist sense, the reality of free will, moral agency, moral culpability, and creativity (which is not to be confused with novelty).[5] But, again, no argument establishing that the sphere of scientific exploration is coterminous with the bounds of reality as yet exists (as widespread and ongoing arguments among philosophers over free will, moral realism, qualia, and consciousness amply illustrate).

To date, partisans of scientism can only point to the incredible success of modern science over the past few centuries in order to justify their claims. This may provide a reason to entertain the possibility that the reality of free will, moral realism, and creative originality that Descartes ascribed to the realm of mind should be rejected, but it is not yet an argument for the truth of such a rejection, let alone a basis for giving such a momentous rejection the status of dogma.

It is both critical and reasonable, then, to distinguish the legitimate contention that the bounds of science are exhausted by the bounds of the physical from the as yet unsubstantiated scientistic claim that the bounds of science are in principle coterminous with the bounds of reality. The first claim, that the bounds of science are delimited by the bounds of the physical, is perfectly acceptable and properly delimits the bounds of science. But the second claim, the scientistic claim, the claim that the bounds of scientific inquiry are coterminous with the bounds of reality, that claim is problematic and unjustified (and, we might note, is a philosophical contention, not a scientific conclusion).

By this point the suppressed premise illicitly empowering scientism is clearly visible. Proponents of scientism are not merely making the

---

5. For an excellent unfolding of the stakes involved in accepting or denying free will, see Kane, *The Significance of Free Will.*

non-problematic claim that realities such as free will, creativity, and agape cannot be detected by science. They are making the unsubstantiated claim that there is no such thing as free will, creativity, moral responsibility, or agape. And they are depending upon a suppressed, unwarranted, *metaphysical* (not methodological) premise: that the bounds of science are coterminous with the bounds of reality.

This metaphysical premise has incredible power in modern Western thought in part because it is so similar to the *methodological* starting point of modern science, and in so many powerful and productive ways we see the world through modern scientific lenses. It is not uncommon for people to think that rejecting the metaphysical claim amounts to rejecting the methodological commitments at the core of modern science.[6] While the validity of the methodology of modern science is beyond question, however, the metaphysical premise, while enormously influential, remains unsubstantiated.

It is logically possible that we are utterly deceived, that we have no free agency, that our perceptions of good and evil are all ultimately indexed to the survival potential of some meme or another, that there is novelty but no creative agency in the universe. *Perhaps* all that is true. But not only has no argument as of yet established any such conclusion to be true, at this point there is simply no good reason to believe it.

Let me re-emphasize that I do not question the accuracy of modern science. I question only the reach of science with regard to the ultimate character of reality. Are scientific conclusions not only accurate but also exhaustive? Is reality as it is visible to modern science not only real but also exhaustive of the real? I answer "no" and "no." But in doing so I bring into question not science but only scientism, only the metaphysical premise that the bounds of science are coterminous with the bounds of reality.

In sum, modern science and modern scientific methodology are clearly established. Thus I affirm the incredible, truth-telling power of modern science. Scientism, on the other hand, if not yet proven false, is not yet established—not even close. It is critical, then, to distinguish science

---

6. In Greenway, "Modern Metaphysics, Dangerous Truth, Post-Moral Ethics," I argue that in important streams of modern Western philosophy, especially in the so-called analytic tradition, the metaphysical premise constitutes a fourth dogma of empiricism, one which remains in place even after, in the wake of the work of W. V. Quine and Donald Davidson, the first three dogmas of empiricism are identified and revealed to be philosophically illegitimate.

from scientism. For while presently it is most rational to affirm modern science, there is no warrant for affirming scientism.

Metaphysical humility

The modern defense of free will was predicated upon Descartes's assertion that reality was ultimately composed of two fundamentally different and distinct types of stuff, the physical and the mental. In humans, according to Descartes, these two types of stuff are both present. Humans have a body and a mind. The empirical sciences are indigenous to the sphere of the body. Free will, moral responsibility, and moral realities are indigenous to the sphere of mind.

I have already commented upon the deleterious effects of Descartes's relegation of all nonhuman creatures wholly to the sphere of the body/machine. What the essence of the influential philosophical position known as materialism, naturalism, physicalism, or scientism amounts to is the relegation of *everything*, including humans, to the sphere of the machine. While Descartes did have contemporaries who held something like this position (e.g., Thomas Hobbes), it was a wholly marginal view. Indeed, in Descartes's time the character of the cosmos was thought to be basically congruent with our ordinary understanding of free will, moral responsibility, and moral reality.

Descartes was distinguished because his work helped to carve out the sphere of material/matter/machine as a distinct sphere where one would only offer explanations in terms of brute causal forces. That is, it was not so much that Descartes carved out the sphere of mind as he carved out the sphere of matter, the scientific sphere in which one sought out prior causes, and wherein explanatory appeal to purposes, goals, or norms was prohibited.[7] In this way, Descartes helped give birth to modern science.

But Descartes affirmed free will, moral responsibility, and moral reality. While he respected the integrity of the sphere of matter (i.e., the sphere of science), he also argued for the sphere of mind. In this respect, my position resembles Descartes's. But I need to stress one critical distinction. Unlike Descartes, I do not claim that ultimate reality is made up of two kinds of stuff (i.e., "substance" in the philosophical sense), the physical and the mental. This dualistic claim is as radically premature as the monistic claim

---

7. This describes the momentous shift from the Aristotelian to the modern Western understanding of causation.

of scientism. No one as yet can be sure about the ultimate character of reality. Accordingly, I do not affirm ontological dualism but contend only that at present it is most reasonable to conclude that our central affirmations in the natural and social sciences as well as in the humanities (including our moral vocabularies) *all*, for the most part, accurately describe real aspects of whatever may be the character of ultimate reality.

Notably, scientism remains essentially Cartesian insofar as it *retains Descartes's basic dualism* and then raises three objections. First, that there is no real need for explanations outside of the sphere of science, for scientific explanation is exhaustively and wholly satisfactory. Second, that explanation indigenous to the realm of mind adds nothing to scientific knowledge. And third, that substance dualism is incoherent because one cannot explain how two radically different types of stuff could interact (the so-called mind/body problem).

None of these objections undercut my position. First, as noted, not even all materialists, let alone all philosophers, agree that explanations from the sphere of the physical can answer or even acknowledge many questions (including all spiritual and moral questions) people find profoundly meaningful. So the contention that scientific explanations can sufficiently account for all the realities of our lives fails. Second, once one distinguishes the realm of science from the realm of the humanities (i.e., study of morality, creative originality, faith), one is not surprised that studies in the humanities do not provide answers to scientific questions or add to scientific knowledge, since by definition that has never been their aim. Third, I confront no mind/body "interaction" problem because I am not asserting mind/body substance dualism. What is the ultimate character of reality? Well, I do not know. But neither does anybody else. And it is sophomoric to deny the reality of free will, moral responsibility, moral reality, and creative originality and to assert scientistic monism in order to avoid saying "I don't know" when in fact no one knows.

In contrast to both Descartes and scientism, my position remains ontologically humble. I do not see as yet any reasonable basis for making totalizing metaphysical claims. Since no one has come close to offering an argument that would compel us to reject free will, moral realism, moral responsibility, and creative originality, and since affirmation of these has proven to be essential to human understanding across cultures and throughout history, it is wholly reasonable to suppose that the ultimate character of

Part Two: Science, Scientism, Morality

reality is best reflected by the rationalities, modalities, and vocabularies of the natural and the human sciences *as well as* by the rationalities, modalities, and vocabularies of the humanities.[8]

Might we over time develop a radically new meta-vocabulary that allows us to forge beyond the present incommensurabilities and address adequately all the realities currently named by our scientific and humanistic/spiritual vocabularies within a single conceptual framework? Perhaps. But if people ever do develop such a vocabulary, then it is most reasonable to expect that by far the essential character of today's central affirmations in the natural and social sciences as well as in the humanities would all be largely preserved. In the meantime, the most reasonable course of action is to continue utilizing that set of vocabularies, incommensurable or no, that together best allow for the fullest and most articulate reflections upon reality.

What would not be reasonable, insofar as, à la Laplace, it would be radically premature, would be to presume that that future, as of yet unimagined conceptual framework is going to be in all essentials identical to today's metaphysical naturalism/materialism (what I am calling scientism).[9] It is wholly reasonable to conclude, then, that we are presently justified in using vocabularies pertinent to and affirming the reality of free will, creative originality, moral reality, and moral responsibility.

While all this should be enough to unseat scientism and its denial of realities such as free will and creative originality, the power of scientistic trajectories in modern Western rationality are so powerful that readers may remain skeptical. For a detailed refutation of scientism see my argument in *A Reasonable Belief: Why God and Faith Make Sense*. Here I will supplement the argument of this chapter with a somewhat technical excursus that exposes the weaknesses of a standard and celebrated defense of scientism, Daniel Dennett's aforementioned *Consciousness Explained* (readers ready to move beyond the debate over scientism are invited to skip ahead to chapter 6).

---

8. Note how the classic *Natur-/Geisteswissenschaften* split subtly but definitively elides this sphere of the humanities, for on either side of the divide one finds only science.

9. Note the congruence of my approach with a "principle of charity" (Donald Davidson) not confined by metaphysical naturalism (as is this same Donald Davidson). That is, to speak very technically for a moment, I would argue that when Davidson asserts anomalous monism fidelity that his own principle of charity is compromised by his unacknowledged commitment to the fourth dogma of empiricism.

Chapter 5

Excursus On the Illusion of an Argument

Daniel Dennett's *Consciousness Explained*

In this excursus I will shore up my defense of free will, creative originality, moral reality, and moral responsibility in the face of celebrated philosopher Daniel Dennett's well-known and influential defense of materialism/physicalism, *Consciousness Explained*.[1] In brief, in *Consciousness Explained*, Dennett uses the potent background climate of modern Western scientism to define his title terms, "consciousness" and "explained," from the start. As a result, by definition the title presumes the conclusion of his argument. In and of itself, to assume the conclusion to his argument for scientism in this fashion (i.e., by building scientistic definitions into the meaning of his title categories) does not necessarily invalidate Dennett's argument. However, since scientism is both the presupposition and the conclusion of Dennett's argument, the only way he can validly establish scientism would be to provide a materialist explanation of consciousness so complete and satisfying that there would remain no space or need for any extraphysical account. I will argue that the conclusiveness Dennett claims for his argument far exceeds his success in any such endeavor.

Dennett's position is called "compatibilist" because he argues that every affirmation we want to make about spiritual realities is compatible with

---

1. Dennett, *Consciousness Explained*.

Part Two: Science, Scientism, Morality

materialism/naturalism/scientism. As noted above, Dennett articulates his fundamental metaphysical contention clearly:

> ... *materialism*: there is only one sort of stuff, namely *matter*— the physical stuff of physics, chemistry, and physiology—and the mind is somehow nothing but a physical phenomenon. In short, the mind is the brain. According to the materialists, we can (in principle!) account for every mental phenomena using the same physical principles, laws, and raw materials that suffice to explain radioactivity, continental drift, photosynthesis, reproduction, nutrition, and growth. It is one of the main burdens of this book to explain consciousness without ever giving in to the siren song of dualism.[2]

In opposition to Dennett's compatibilism, defenders of consciousness and "free will" in the classic sense are called "incompatibilists" because they argue that our classic affirmations of such spiritual realities are incompatible with materialism, but are also significant and real. Clearly, classic spiritual realities are *not* compatible with materialism. Dennett does not deny this. But he rejects our ordinary and classic views about spiritual realities. To the contrary, he considers them confused relics of a bygone age. Henceforth, he argues, whatever we mean by these terms (e.g., creative originality, good, evil, moral responsibility, freedom [i.e., freedom from external constraint; by contrast, free will must be rejected as an incoherent idea]) should be understood within materialist confines. It is these revised understandings that Dennett thinks we should find fully satisfactory in accounting for every aspect of life.

Since, again, Dennett presumes the conclusion he is setting out to prove, the only way for his argument to succeed in a valid fashion would be if his explanations were so complete and satisfying that no one any longer saw any need to question their completeness. But this is famously and indisputably not the case. Indeed, even many philosophers and scientists who share Dennett's naturalistic commitments and applaud his efforts conclude that a fully scientific understanding requires us to face the hard truth that much that humans treasure in classic affirmations of spiritual realities must be abandoned.

In the context of philosophy's free will controversies this position is so significant that it names the third major school of thought in the debate over the reality of free will: "hard determinism." "Hard determinists" are

---

2. Ibid., 33.

Excursus On the Illusion of an Argument

materialists who argue that spiritual realities name distinct and treasured possibilities, but think these spiritual realities are incompatible with materialism and so must, unfortunately, be rejected. That is, even among fellow materialists, let alone among those who affirm spiritual realities, Dennett's compatibilism remains unconvincing.

In short, this can be said quite certainly: no one has established the truth of scientism. In the final paragraph of his lengthy argument, even Dennett acknowledges the obvious, "My explanation of consciousness is far from complete. One might even say that it was just a beginning, but it *is* a beginning, because it breaks the spell of the enchanted circle of ideas that made explaining consciousness seem impossible."[3] Of course, luminaries like Descartes and Kant, along with a multitude of other first-rate philosophical minds East and West from antiquity to the present have concluded, speaking roughly, that any adequate account of consciousness must invoke categories indigenous to what Descartes called the sphere of mind. For all of them, the most obvious conclusion to be drawn from one of the world's foremost defenders of scientism's 468-page failure to provide anything close to a complete explanation of consciousness would be confirmation that Dennett so far provides us no reason to think that consciousness can be wholly accounted for within materialist parameters. This is a clear and sober conclusion, not an indication that anyone who draws such a conclusion must be bewitched by the "spell" of some "enchanted circle of ideas."

These facts alone justify the conclusion that one can quite reasonably and confidently affirm science, reject scientism, and affirm spiritual realities. But this bare philosophical response is not likely to feel adequate in the face of *Consciousness Explained*. This is not because rejection of scientism is irrational, but because aside from his unsuccessful effort to establish the wholesale adequacy of materialistic explanation, Dennett launches invalid attacks with real rhetorical power. The power of the attacks does not stem from the validity of Dennett's argument. It stems from the ubiquity of a background scientistic consensus. This is the subtle but potent consensus uncovered in the illicit nature/nurture and/or.

For instance, Dennett raises the mind-body problem as a major obstacle for those who reject scientism. The "*very idea* of . . . a locus of mind-brain interaction," Dennett stresses, is so problematic that neither Descartes "nor any subsequent dualist has ever overcome it convincingly."[4]

---

3. Ibid., 455.
4. Ibid., 41, 33.

This sure sounds significant. However, unless one surreptitiously slips in this premise, "and anything that we cannot presently understand using a single rationality/vocabulary must be false," not even the existence of an unresolved mind-body problem would do anything to make Dennett's case.

Moreover, once one has dropped the premature Cartesian assertion of ontological dualism, the positive force of Dennett's objection reduces to pointing out that no one can as yet provide *under a single rationality* an account that explains both material and spiritual realities. In reduced form this is no objection at all, for it merely articulates the position defended here, which is precisely that no single rationality satisfactorily accounts for all areas of understanding and reality. Might people someday develop such an all-inclusive, single rationality? Perhaps. What is certain is that none of this amounts to an objection to classic affirmations of spiritual realities. It does not follow from "you have no single rationality . . ." that "you must now affirm scientism."

With even more rhetorical power, Dennett uses a background scientistic consensus to inscribe scientism wholesale into our understanding of "consciousness" and "explanation." In outlining his approach to consciousness, for instance, Dennett suggests that we think in terms of "intentional stances," that is, that we treat a, "noise-emitter [e.g., a human] as an agent, indeed a rational agent, who harbors beliefs and desires and other mental states that exhibit *intentionality* or 'aboutness,' and whose actions can be explained (or predicted) on the basis of the content of these states."[5] He insists that we remain "neutral" about the consciousness of the "noise-emitter," which we do by ascribing to the noise-emitter not consciousness but only an "intentional stance." To carry out a proper investigation, Dennett argues, one needs to maintain this "neutrality" while "devising and confirming an empirical theory that could in principle vindicate the subjects."[6]

However, since by definition "an empirical theory" about a "noise-emitter" with "an intentional stance" could only vindicate materialists like Dennett, there is nothing neutral about any of this. Indeed, insofar as Dennett defines the "intentional stance" as a publicly observable "aboutness" relation between a nonconscious subject (i.e., a "noise-emitter") and reality, that is, as an empirical relationship explicated within wholly materialist parameters that presume wholly and only a physicalist subject-object relationship, there is in principle no possible way anyone thinking solely in

---

5. Ibid., 76.
6. Ibid., 83.

Excursus On the Illusion of an Argument

terms of intentional stances could ever come to affirm any spiritual reality. Here, then, one sees the very materialism Dennett is arguing for built into the purportedly neutral framework he insists we adopt before engaging in the argument itself.

Again, if Dennett were to make clear that he is presuming his conclusion in his premises and then depend upon the utterly complete and satisfying character of his explanation to avoid the accusation of illicit circular argument, there would be no problem (well, it would be a problem for Dennett's argument, since at the end of his book he acknowledges that he is not remotely close to providing a complete explanation). The claim of neutrality, however, is illicit. And to the degree any conclusions Dennett draws depend upon the claim to neutrality, to that degree he is indeed guilty of arguing in a circle (i.e., to that degree he is guilty of presuming his own answer to the question at issue).

In a subtler but equally problematic rhetorical move, Dennett uses the intentional stance to prejudice his engagement with his most significant non-materialist opponents, twentieth-century phenomenologists. The non-neutral character of Dennett's "intentional stance" framing of the issue is obvious if, unlike Dennett in *Consciousness Explained*, one enters into conversation with an actual phenomenologist. Consider, for instance, this account of consciousness from Emmanuel Levinas. Note how Levinas, who writes before Dennett but who is responding to the classic, twentieth-century "consciousness is an intentional stance" scientistic trajectory that Dennett is taking up, draws a distinction between the classic, spiritual notion of consciousness (what he calls "non-intentional consciousness") in contrast to materialist aspects of consciousness (what he calls "intentional consciousness"):

> a consciousness directed at the world and its objects, structured as intentionality, is also *indirectly*, and supplementarily, as it were, consciousness of itself: consciousness of the active self that represents the world and objects to itself, as well as consciousness of its very acts of representation, consciousness of mental activity. But it would be an indirect consciousness: immediate, but without an intentional aim; implicit and purely of accompaniment. Nonintentional, to be distinguished from the inner perception into which it would be apt to be converted [e.g., the "introspection" of Dennett's heterophenomenology]. The latter, reflective consciousness, takes the self, its states, and its mental acts *as objects*: reflective consciousness, in which consciousness directed toward the world

seeks help in overcoming the inevitable naivete of its intentional rectilinearity, forgetful of the indirect *vecu* [literally: "lived"] of the nonintentional and its horizons, forgetful of what accompanies it.[7]

Since Levinas is one of the most prominent of the phenomenologists whom Dennett claims to be taking on, and since Levinas explicitly distinguishes intentional consciousness of the sort Dennett presumes in his supposedly "neutral" starting point, from the *non-intentional* consciousness which is the subject of ordinary and classic understandings of consciousness, it is clear that Dennett's insistence that in order to be neutral we must investigate consciousness beginning from an intentional stance and looking for empirical confirmation, utterly fails to address the real challenge of phenomenologists and predetermines that any conclusions he will draw from the scientific studies that fill the next several hundred pages of his "argument" will confirm his materialism. Dennett makes glancing reference to the problem posed by the actual understanding of phenomenologists, conceding that it "would always be open for someone to insist . . . that the real phenomenological items *accompanied* the goings-on without being identical to them, but whether or not this claim would carry conviction is another matter."[8] In fact, whether or not this claim carries conviction *is precisely the matter* (after all, this is *precisely* Levinas's claim). But apart from this brief aside Dennett fails utterly to address it. Instead, confirming our suspicions, he immediately moves to describe how a primitive robot named SHAKEY in the 1960s was able to identify and manipulate a box. This, for Dennett, is a neutral example of a noise-emitter adopting what we could describe empirically as an intentional stance.

SHAKEY is very interesting, but insofar as phenomenologists like Levinas are neither claiming that SHAKEY is conscious nor denying that SHAKEY's computer processing may be in part similar to the processing that goes on in our brain, it is utterly irrelevant to the argument. Dennett, however, convinced that his empirical investigation of our "intentional stance" constitutes a "neutral method for investigating and describing phenomenology," dedicates the next couple of hundred pages of the book to the "empirical theory of consciousness itself" and to philosophical

---

7. Levinas, *entre-nous*, 127–28.
8. Dennett, *Consciousness Explained*, 85.

"problems of consciousness."[9] The empirical theory turns out to be a few hundred pages of more advanced SHAKEY-type stories. It is fascinating and enjoyable reading. It certainly does help us understand how our brains work and insofar as our consciousness is conditioned and constrained by empirical reality it gives us important information (recall that we do not deny the influence or significance of nature or nurture). But none of this does anything to establish the truth of materialism or to disprove the reality of *non-intentional* consciousness. That is to say, none of this disproves the reality of spiritual realities as ordinarily and classically conceived.

In Dennett's "philosophical problems" section, likewise, the die has already been cast. Proponents of spiritual realities are rejected because their positions require rejection of scientism, that is, because they are unable to offer explanations without appealing to non-materialist explanation, and/or because they fail to answer scientific questions (scientific questions that, note well, they were never attempting to answer in the first place). That is, they are rejected because they fail to add anything scientific and material to our explanatory quiver. They are dismissed because their positions are not intelligible within the materialist confines Dennett presumes. But since the explanatory reach of scientistic materialism is itself the question under debate, to criticize explanations because they are not in accord with scientific materialism is a textbook example of the fallacy of begging the question (i.e., of presuming the truth of one's conclusions in one's premises).

But, someone may object, what explanation of spiritual realities can we defenders of spiritual realities provide? It is all well and good to criticize Dennett for failing to provide a wholly satisfying explanation, one might object, but does not that objection ring hollow absent a better explanation? To the degree that this objection seems forceful, one has been captured by a question-begging, empiricist definition of "explanation." Descartes, among numerous other philosophers, could also, just like Dennett, have labeled some of his work "Consciousness Explained." Of course, his explanation would have been radically different from Dennett's insofar as he would have stipulated that the explanation of consciousness, while it might invoke categories from within the sphere of matter, would need also to invoke categories indigenous to the sphere of mind.

Dennett rejects out of hand any such Cartesian explanation of consciousness, however, for when Dennett demands an *explanation* he is demanding an explanation in the scientific, empirical sense appropriate to

9. Ibid., 98.

the sphere of matter. Precisely there, with that implicit demand that any explanation be empirical, Dennett inserts his materialist conclusion into the initial definition of "explanation." When Dennett uses "explained" in the title, *Consciousness Explained*, he is already presuming that explanation equals naturalistic/materialist/scientistic explanation. So one is left with an either/or that excludes extra-naturalistic explanation from the beginning: *either* we can explain consciousness in wholly materialist terms *or* no explanation of consciousness is possible. This either/or prejudices the question by simply rendering invisible the position of his opponents: explanation of consciousness requires extra-materialist categories. The real and legitimate either/or would be framed thus: *either* we can explain consciousness in entirely materialist terms *or* explanation of consciousness requires extra-materialist categories. Dennett's either/or, by contrast, illicitly renders his opponent's position invisible by presupposing his own scientistic naturalism/materialism on both sides of the either/or.

Dennett's either/or means that with regard to explaining consciousness we will either be successful in offering materialist explanation of consciousness or we will face defeat in our attempt to explain consciousness. According to Dennett, then, those who affirm spiritual realities are people who "are tempted by the *defeatist* thesis that science couldn't 'in principle' explain the various 'mysteries' of the mind."[10] "Such *defeatism*, today," Dennett says, "in the midst of a cornucopia of scientific advances ready to be exploited, strikes me as ludicrous, even pathetic, but I suppose it could be the sad truth."[11]

Insofar as "explanation" of consciousness in Dennett's sense would entail rejection of free will, good, evil, moral responsibility, and creative originality, his apportioning of potential "sadness" is striking, because many people (including, by definition, his fellow scientific materialists, the hard determinists) are indeed saddened by the potential loss of these spiritual realities. Moreover, there is reason to be wary of Dennett's enthusiastic pairing of "scientific advances" with talk of "exploitation," especially when moral reality in the classic sense is simultaneously being rejected.

Finally, when Dennett equates "explanation" with "empirical/materialist explanation" he obliterates any possible distinction between science and scientism. This illicit equating of science and scientism allows him unjustifiably to equate opposition to scientism with opposition to science. In

10. Ibid., 15, emphasis mine.
11. Ibid., 40, emphasis mine.

Excursus On the Illusion of an Argument

the terms of his argument here, it allows him to cast those who contend that consciousness cannot be explained using wholly materialist categories (i.e., anyone who disagrees with his materialism) as being against science. That is, because he illicitly presumes materialism when he invokes "explanation," Dennett can cast himself as the defender of science and illicitly cast his opponents as enemies of science.

Dennett takes all these illicit philosophical moves and combines them with what is essentially name-calling to great rhetorical effect:

> There is the lurking suspicion that the most attractive feature of mind stuff is its promise of being *so* mysterious that it keeps science at bay forever. [Paragraph break.] This fundamentally antiscientific stance of dualism is, to my mind, its most disqualifying feature, and is the reason why in this book I adopt the apparently dogmatic rule that dualism is to be avoided *at all costs*. It is not that I can give a knock-down proof that dualism, in all its forms, is false or incoherent, but that, given the way dualism wallows in mystery, *accepting dualism is giving up*.[12]

In short, here is the either/or Dennett illicitly sets up: *either* (the optimistic, can-do option) we can explain consciousness in wholly scientific terms *or* (the defeatist option) we are too dense to attain unto an explanation. Another alternative, the idea that consciousness cannot be explained fully in scientific categories because it deals with nonempirical realities, and thus properly falls in part within the sphere of the humanities, is eliminated as an option not only *without argument but without even appearing as a possible position*. For Dennett, *either* consciousness can be explained using wholly materialist categories (and so does not exist in the classic sense) *or* explanation of consciousness is beyond our capacities to understand (and we are left wallowing in mystery, sad and defeated). That is, the critical question about the character of consciousness is begged from the first, while sheer name-calling is dressed up in the guise of responsible philosophical argument.

To be clear, there would be no problem if the title of the book were *Consciousness Insofar as It Can Be Naturalistically Explained*. With regard to a more recent work of Dennett's, *Breaking the Spell: Religion as a Natural Phenomena*, there would be no problem if the title were *Religion Insofar as It Is a Natural Phenomena*, where one understands in principle that spiritual realities can never be fully explained by science. Indeed, I can affirm

12. Ibid., 37.

Part Two: Science, Scientism, Morality

all of the *scientific* conclusions of *Consciousness Explained* with the proviso that I am affirming good science, not scientism. There is no reason to deny the accuracy of modern science. There is only reason to contest the unsubstantiated claim that materialist explanation is not only accurate but also exhaustive. In short, one should affirm science but reject scientism.

In summary, both the "consciousness" and the "explained" in *Consciousness Explained* are from the start defined and understood within wholly materialist parameters. In one sense, this is entirely unsurprising, for the character of the investigation precludes the possibility of a neutral starting point. Materialism has been the preeminent presupposition and goal of study in the modern Western natural and social sciences (and it has considerable sway even in the humanities). As I have been careful to concede, this does not mean that materialists presuppose their conclusions (i.e., beg the question, *merely* unfold a tautology, argue in a vicious circle). But it does mean, again, that their position is warranted only to the degree that all reasonable inquirers find materialist explanation wholly satisfying—and that is not even close to being the case.

In *Consciousness Explained*, Dennett gives his position unwarranted standing by explicitly and illicitly claiming that his materialist starting point is neutral and objective. Thus he discerns no significant issue in his failure actually to offer wholly satisfactory materialist accounts of spiritual realities. Moreover, his purportedly "neutral" framework actually requires that the framing not merely of any possible explanations but of any meaningful questions will be materialist. This allows him to dismiss those who affirm spiritual realities by citing their failure to raise empirical questions and their inability to provide empirical explanations. With these conceptual moves, Dennett *does* fallaciously presuppose his conclusions (i.e., begs the question, merely unfolds a tautology, argues in a vicious circle). Among the host of intellectuals who have absorbed twentieth-century materalism/naturalism/scientism and who take its premises as an unquestionable given, the conclusions of *Consciousness Explained* are already implicit in their understanding of "consciousness" and "explained." As a consequence, the book's conclusions can seem very powerful indeed, and the poverty of the actual argument and the influential role of the prejudicial rhetoric can pass by largely unnoticed.

When realities such as free will or having been seized (i.e., moral reality) are referenced, reductionistic scientists and philosophers—and, again, that is not to say all scientists and philosophers, perhaps not even a majority, but *reductionistic/materialist* scientists and philosophers—will point out that these categories make no sense and thus deserve no place within our modern picture of the world. This argument has no force for those affirming free will and moral reality, for defenders of free will and moral reality affirm that precisely these realities are outside the conceptual parameters of modern science and point out that because these realities lie outside of the conceptual parameters of modern science, modern science by definition cannot see them.

Those with a passion for scientism can get a bit reactionary over the suggestion that science is not able, in principle, to give complete and exhaustive explanations for every aspect of reality and life. One sometimes hears proponents of scientism lament that to admit that there may be any break in the material, deterministic/indeterministic causal continuum is to ruin science. As should now be clear, to posit such a break, to name the methodological limitations of science, to affirm in the classic and ordinary sense consciousness, free will, moral agency, moral reality, and creative originality, to deny that the parameters of empirical investigation are not coterminous with the parameters of reality: none of this ruins science. What it quite properly and on the basis of responsible philosophical argument does do is deny the patently unwarranted and hegemonic assertions of scientism.

This argument supports the judgment reached at the end of the last chapter: there is good reason to affirm science but no good reason to affirm scientism. Quite reasonably, then, I affirm science but reject scientism. This means, as I will discuss in the next chapter, that one can affirm both science and, in the classic and ordinary sense, affirm moral realism.

Chapter 6

Affirming Science *and* Moral Realism

Affirming science and moral realism

The predominance of the natural and social sciences in modern Western society means that many Westerners tend to be educated into a scientistic conception of reality by default. It is rare for textbooks and teachers in the natural and social sciences to say explicitly that their empirical methodologies render significant aspects of reality inaccessible. For instance, many Westerners are simply taught the empirical nature/nurture and/or as if it exhausted all explanatory options, thereby eliding, definitively, surreptitiously, and illicitly (and often unwittingly), free will, creativity, moral responsibility, good, evil, and the possibility of any divinity. Again, I am not calling into question the accuracy of the findings of the modern natural and social sciences. It is only the scientistic claim that is problematic.

Recall the concern, joy, sadness, and horror by which I hope you were seized as you read the stories about Kiki, the cricket, the seal, and the orca. These moral responses are surely manifest in the chemistry and reactions taking place in our brains (and, perhaps, throughout the rest of our bodies as well). Moreover, there is every reason to think that occasions of having been seized could be, did we possess enough knowledge, artificially stimulated by impulses of some sort delivered by probes directly to certain parts of our brain. It is even possible, science fiction style (e.g., *The Matrix*, *Star Trek*'s "holodeck"), to suppose that we could be deceived into thinking we are having real reactions to a real reality when in fact we are reacting to brain probes or contrived realities. Nonetheless, all that this establishes is that we humans are material beings and that we can be deceived; it does not establish that as material beings our having been seized by love for Faces or our always after-the-fact sense of having freely willed is always or usually false.

There is no reason to suspect humans are caught in some matrix of deception. There is no reason as yet to affirm the wholesale materialism/physicalism of scientism. Whatever the ultimate character of existence, it is metaphysically humble and eminently reasonable at present to suppose that the vocabularies of the natural and social sciences *and also* the vocabularies of the humanities and of spirituality *are all* largely true.

In daily life and experience, as people choose relatively freely among options, as they feel pride, guilt, joy, or horror, as they love and sacrifice, create new ideas, and judge people morally culpable, as they do all these things they live out and affirm in the most significant and profound dimensions of their lives aspects of a reality beyond the parameters of science. That is, in daily life most everyone in fact lives out affirmations of free will and moral reality. So the reductionism implicit in the natural and social sciences is hardly the only real and significant influence upon our philosophies of life and, let me emphasize, many (perhaps most) scientists do not affirm scientism (i.e., Dennett-style materialism).

Let me reiterate that I am not denying the profound influence of nature and nurture, I am only denying that nature and nurture taken together offer comprehensive categories of explanation; on that point the burden of proof rests squarely upon those who would deny free will, moral reality, moral culpability, and genuine creativity. That burden of proof is presently not even close to having been met. All one finds so far are LaPlace-style hasty extrapolations.

The modern assault upon moral realism, free will, and moral responsibility is so vehemently asserted by many mainstream intellectual trajectories that I will tarry upon this point for one more moment in an attempt to make the stakes of this discussion brutally vivid, and the significance of our affirmation of classic moral realism unmistakable. I use a horrifying example. I do this because somehow it is over and against the brute edge of evil that spiritual reality is most obvious.

This mental video clip will be familiar and, unfortunately, you most likely will be able to bring many similar clips to mind. A family of five,

PART TWO: SCIENCE, SCIENTISM, MORALITY

mother, father, two older sisters, and a young brother holding a teddy bear are lined up with a few other families facing a ditch. Behind them are Nazi soldiers with machine guns. The video clips I have seen lack sound. The guns jerk in the soldiers' hands and bodies buckle and crumple into the earth.

Let's go straight to the point with a blunt question: when you see those murders, what is most real and significant, the fact that the guns are made of steel, the biology of the bodies, the physics of the falls into the ditch, the social, historical, and psychological dynamics that led to those soldiers being in that situation and pulling those triggers, or the reality of the evil, the horrible violation?

It is perfectly legitimate to brace oneself against this story as one begins to sense what is coming. My apology was meant sincerely, though obviously I still thought the point so important that it warranted using this disturbing and, notably, real-life modern Western example. What is not legitimate, however, is to think that one is bracing oneself against what is merely emotional and subjective and so not really real, and to think that such bracing denial of moral reality is part of what is required if one is to consider this event in a serious, scholarly, intellectual, or rigorous fashion.

To be sure, there is a place for strictly scientific analysis of dimensions of this event, and scientists studying the event in the role of sociologist or historian may need to distance themselves methodologically from the heinous, moral dimension of the event in order to achieve important scientific ends. If done self-consciously, for good reasons and only *partially* (i.e., the researchers retain contact with moral reality, with having been seized), then there is no need to object to such objectifying study.

But what is not legitimate and is indeed morally repugnant and socially dangerous is to deny wholly and in principle the extra-natural reality of the evil, to deny that reality because it does not fit within the methodological and ontological confines of modern scientific inquiry. That would be an attempt to eliminate what is most real and significant in the event: the terror, the evil, the moral culpability, the emotional pain of those mothers and fathers and children and the transforming reality of their love for one another, as well as our emotional pain and moral horror as we witness and remember. Such wholesale denial of the monstrous violation of those people would itself be evil. It would also be dangerous, for insofar as it involves a blunting and attempted denial of our primordial, moral, having been seized, it leaves us primed to deny moral reality generally and to facilitate other evils.

Again, to object in this way is anti-scientism, not antiscientific. This event is not only susceptible to natural and social scientific analysis but, insofar as the actions of the soldiers were highly conditioned by the realities of nature and nurture, scientific analysis is absolutely critical if we are to attempt to understand important factors that foster such evil actions. Scientific analysis is important because it will play a role as we work to lessen the possibility of the recurrence of such events. In particular, the psychological, social, and political forces visible to empirical analysis are real factors contributing to such events, and we understand such events more fully and can forestall recurrence of such events more effectively with solid scientific understanding.

Not even vis-à-vis such significant and horrifying moral events, then, am I denying the validity, significance, and potentially profound benefits of modern science and the value of adopting a properly scientific stance of detachment. However, against the grain of predominant streams of modern Western rationality, I am vitally concerned to make clear that the reality that is most real, significant, and influential, namely, the having been seized that led some heroic Germans to resist their own leaders and nation despite mortal danger to themselves: this reality is not visible to science. In other words, the reality that often motivates scientific investigation and typically leads people to judge science important and valuable—for instance, people value the discovery of the polio vaccine because it has prevented awful suffering and loss for so many children—this reality, *moral reality*, is *by definition not visible to science as such*. One cannot put on empirical spectacles and see moral reality. To the contrary, empirical spectacles elide moral reality by definition and design.[1]

What is both common among contemporary Western intellectuals and ridiculous is to put on empirical spectacles, look around, see no spiritual reality, and proffer as a scientific or philosophical conclusion that there is no spiritual reality. Chemists, physicists, biologists, psychologists, social psychologists, and sociologists can see many different realities, can make critical contributions to life, can be moral persons, but they cannot via their

---

1. Notably, because we are physical creatures it is also possible that physical factors could impede or even cut off our ability to discern or be seized by moral reality. Just as certain chemicals can render us deaf or blind, chemicals that interfered, for instance, with normal reactions involving oxytocin in the body might degrade or cut off our moral capacities.

various scientific disciplines see moral reality or deduce moral truths, and they are not by virtue of their expertise in their various scientific disciplines specially qualified to make metaphysical claims or ethical judgments.[2]

This decisive difference between scientific and moral reality explains why in exploring moral reality I do not engage in scientific reflection. Instead, I share stories that appeal to having been seized by love for the Faces of humans, seals, orcas, cats, crickets, and saplings (i.e., stories that appeal to agape). Only in such fashion does moral reality become visible. When we find ourselves seized by moral reality, then good, evil, responsibility, and the moral being of others and ourselves are all manifest and influential. After the fact, reflectively, we can identify and name these realities. Initially they seize us with an immediacy that is prior to reflection, prior to our control, prior to our grasping of them. For instance, you do not *decide* to be horrified by the evil of that Nazi killing field. Rather, you find yourself seized by the horror of the violation of those Faces, for you are seized immediately and before making any decision by those Faces; you are immediately traumatized by the horrific violation of those Faces.

Responsibility and Response-Ability

In reflecting and deciding you can name and describe and act in accord with or in resistance to primordial, moral, having been seized, but you do not straightaway determine or originate your having been seized. Primordial, moral, having been seized cannot be defined into existence, deduced from self-evident principles, or detected through a microscope. You must engage in some living encounter, or the narrative of such, wherein you find yourself morally seized. We realize, then, that the ordinary moral vocabulary of *responsibility* is both revealing and precise, for we discern moral reality precisely in our *response* to such situations or narratives. That is, it is

---

2. While most scientists (not to mention virtually all ethicists and philosophers) would concur with these distinctions, a vocal minority—most famously the best-selling author Sam Harris (*The Moral Landscape*)—has recently been insisting that science can deliver ethical truth. Speaking technically for a moment, I would note in brief that Harris utterly fails to discern the force of G. E. Moore's "open question" argument or, as essentially the same problem is otherwise articulated, the challenge of Henry Sidgwick's "dualism of practical reason." For a far more sophisticated response to Moore and Sidgwick, see Katarzyna de Lazari-Radek and Peter Singer, *The Point of View of the Universe*. For a discussion of the relationship between the agape ethics I am defending here and de Lazari-Radek and Singer's utilitarian ethics, see Greenway, "Peter Singer, Emmanuel Levinas, Christian Agape, and the Spiritual Heart of Animal Liberation."

in our sense of responsibility that our response-*ability* is, indirectly, manifest. Responsibility is the immediate consequence of the response-ability manifest in having been seized. If one must use "sense perception" type language, one could say that in the response-ability conveying responsibility our "moral sense" is manifest. Responsibility follows immediately upon response-ability, a capacity manifest in our responses, in our having been seized by love for others, a having been seized that in diverse circumstances results in horror, joy, grief, gratitude, respect, awe, happiness, mourning, regret, hope, or angst.

Our free agency can also be delineated vis-à-vis response-ability and responsibility. Since response-ability is only indirectly discernable, that is, discernable after the fact, we cannot directly choose to see something as good or as evil. We find ourselves seized by concern for others before any possibility of direct choice. We do, however, possess significant freedom vis-à-vis responsibility. For instance, in the face of evil you might act to heighten your sensitivities and attentiveness and act valiantly or, on the other hand, you might blunt your sensitivities and turn away, perhaps in selfishness or in cowardice. Over time, if you habitually blunt moral sensitivities and cultivate selfishness or cowardice, you might succeed in severely dampening your response-ability. In other words, over time you may succeed in dampening your moral sensitivity (i.e., you may succeed in hardening your heart). On the other hand, if you cultivate attentiveness and valiant action, you may heighten your moral sensitivities and maximize courage and strength for good action.

I am not suggesting an inerrant moral sense. I am not suggesting that with regard to ethical quandaries we can apprehend directly and without question what is right. There is no magical shortcut to resolving ethical quandary cases. But the inability to answer every ethical question with certainty is not a basis for rejecting moral reality wholesale. Nor is it a basis for questioning the truth of classic moral judgments that are not at all ambiguous (e.g., the evil perpetuated by that Nazi firing squad, or the realization that greed is evil). To the degree that there is no ethical ambiguity we should judge, act, and in some cases legislate with proportionate confidence. To the degree that there is ethical ambiguity, proportional humility over our ethical judgments and restraint vis-à-vis legislation is likewise appropriate.

The fact that science can never fully measure or describe moral realities as such has nothing to do with any scientific shortcoming or failure. There is no reason to conclude that if we develop a better scientific method or more accurate means of measuring, then spiritual realities may be exhaustively described and measured. It is not the case even in principle that ultimately agape can be better or more fully expressed with a scientific description or mathematical equation. To the contrary, the vocabularies and rationality of science are not the optimal vocabularies we might use to describe or communicate, for instance, our love or moral horror.

Because scientific language is neither the most powerful nor the most accurate vocabulary with which to express spiritual realities, these realities and the awakening of people to them has classically been the task of poetry, literature, painting, music, and, notably, theological and religious work composed and interpreted in the modality of the humanities, for these are the rationalities, vocabularies, and modalities through which spiritual realities are most accurately made manifest and reflected upon (so, no more stabs at a *science* of morals or a *science* of God).

It is through poetry, literature, film, music, dance, and the like that these realities—love, joy, moral horror, grief—become manifest. We know too that these realities, the realities of love, goodness, and evil, which science cannot directly see, are the most profound realities of all. But they are only manifest when we encounter life in the modality of the humanities. The stories I tell, then, are not decorative digressions I throw in to keep things entertaining. The stories are essential to my argument. For it is only when one writes in a narrative mode that moral realities come into view.

To be clear, I am not criticizing modern science. I am criticizing a philosophical confusion that haunts not only science but also modern Western rationality. Notably, while I bring modern philosophical claims *about* science into question, I do not challenge any particular scientific discoveries. My target is not the experimental conclusions of any particular modern science (astronomy, biology, chemistry, physics, hydrology, social psychology, sociology, and so forth), but a powerful reductionistic trajectory in modern philosophy, a trajectory that has been illicitly presented as scientific. I reject only the illegitimate and hegemonic claim that, in principle, modern science can discern *all* that is real.

Likewise, I am not doing science. I expect most all readers know what it is to identify an empirical question, develop a hypothesis, set up tests that will support or invalidate the hypothesis, and so forth. Most all of us know when we are doing chemistry or physics or social psychology. But while I am dependent upon scientific knowledge (e.g., from discussion of modern astronomy to discussion of the relation of emotions to cellular chemistry),

Affirming Science and Moral Realism

my argument is not scientific but philosophical and, wholly reasonably, built upon awakening to spiritual realities.

A PHYSICIST'S TALE

Professor Alan Lightman, a physicist at MIT and a best-selling author (*Einstein's Dreams*; *Mr g: A Novel About Creation*), is an atheist. In essays published in Salon.com, "Does God exist?" and "Why atheists should respect believers," however, Lightman criticizes "the anti-religion of Richard Dawkins" and defends the "case for reconciling the scientific with the divine."[3] At the very end of "Does God exist?" Lightman shares a personal story that is presumably a major part of the reason why, despite his atheism, he is interested in preserving the possibility of some sort of affirmation of spiritual reality.

Lightman recounts a stunning encounter with two baby ospreys. The baby ospreys' nest was a short distance from his back porch, and Lightman began watching them through binoculars when they hatched in early June. One August afternoon, Lightman was watching when the ospreys, who had apparently been watching Lightman right back, took off on their maiden flight. Eventually, Lightman says, the ospreys flew in a large loop around his house. Then they pivoted and dove straight for him at tremendous speed, freezing him in place and making direct eye contact before pulling up and away at the last moment. "Words cannot convey," Lightman writes in the closing lines of his essay, "what was exchanged between us in that instant .... After they were gone, I found that I was shaking, and in tears. To this day I cannot explain what happened in that half-second. But it was one of the most profound moments of my life."[4]

I hope that my argument makes clear why we can celebrate and affirm the spiritual reality of Lightman's encounter without compromising upon reason or the integrity of modern Western science. I hope that by this point it is clear how influential understandings of modern philosophy, science, and even modern Christian theology cut humans off from other creatures. I also hope that by this point it is clear that for the sake of humans and all creatures, we can wholly reasonably retrieve a lost source of spiritual

---

3. Lightman, "Does God Exist?" Find a response from Dennett in "When atheists fib to protect God," and Lightman's retort in "Why atheists should respect believers." Lightman later develops his ideas in *The Accidental Universe*.

4. Lightman, "Does God Exist?"

comfort and joy, a lost sense of belonging to this world, a lost realization that life, all life, is sacred. My hope is that we will open ourselves ever more fully to the passion of agape, that is, to having been seized by love for all Faces.

Although I hope I have stimulated reawakening to moral reality and to passion for the good, let me stress challenges that immediately arise and confront any reinvigorating of passion on the moral plane: to reopen oneself to passion is to play with fire, for there is very real potential for moral passion to become explosive, oppressive, and/or irrational. It is critical, then, that I explicitly delimit the character, strengths, and dangers of an appeal to moral passion. That is the critical task I now take up. I argue that despite my move beyond objectivity and my contention that the passion of agape lies at the heart of ethics, the dangers of ethical relativism and ethical extremism can be contained. Explaining this is the task of "Part Three: Beyond Objectivity, Relativism and Extremism: Moral Realism, Ethical Surety, and the Sanctity of Life."

I also erase the bright moral line typically drawn between humans and other creatures. In an age when humans themselves are increasingly being turned into instrumental commodities and exploited, many may fear that erasing this bright moral line undercuts the moral standing of humans. This concern should fade insofar as readers realize that in the predominant streams of modern Western thought I am criticizing, moral realism itself is rejected. I defend moral realism and agape ethics, and this amounts to a defense of the moral standing of *all* creatures, humans included. Nonetheless, erasure of a clean moral line between humans and other species raises complicated questions about "moral status." Addressing these questions will be the task of "Part Four: Perfect Love in an Imperfect World: Agape Ethics."

Part Three

BEYOND OBJECTIVITY, RELATIVISM, AND EXTREMISM
Moral Realism, Ethical Surety, and the Sanctity of Life

Chapter 7

Against Ethical Relativism

Modern ethics' scientistic demand

As is by this point clear, my argument says a deliberate "no" to what in modernity became an ideal for ethical argument, namely, "no" to the demand for a rational system that begins dispassionately from objective and logically indubitable (i.e., certain) first principles. Because of the character of primordial, moral, having been seized by love for all Faces, I avoid formulating ethical arguments in accord with the modern ideal.

People who embrace the modern ideal demand just such an argument. They demand a "prove to me from objective, indubitable premises that you're right" argument. They say until I do that I offer nothing more than opinion. When people make this modern ethical demand what they insist upon, often unwittingly, is that we disregard having been seized by love for all Faces. What they demand is that we suppress the truth of human having been seized by love for all creatures, that we deny the moral passions that fire any truly ethical convictions (including those having to do with human Faces).

Such folk are bewitched by modernity, for modern Western rationality encourages them to understand themselves as rigorous, neutral, and open, imposing only the most minimal demands of rationality, waiting only to be convinced by an objective argument. Such is the innocent mask cloaking a dagger to the heart of ethics that is concealed in the modern demand that ethical arguments be objective and logically indubitable. In fact, ethical arguments are at root intrinsically subjective and impassioned, for they are rooted not in reason, but in agape.[1]

The modern ethical ideal, witting or unwitting, is unconscionable. There is nothing neutral about the demand that one neutralize primordial, moral, having been seized by love for Faces (i.e., agape). In the wake of that demand, influential modern and postmodern paradigms elide moral reality altogether. In many modern and postmodern paradigms the moral has long since been absorbed by the aesthetic (e.g., the good has been reduced to what one desires or prefers), or the moral has been equated with enlightened self-interest (which remains nonmoral insofar as it ultimately pivots upon self-interest), or the moral has been dissolved into genetic and sociocultural conditioning (e.g., when biology's group, kinship and/or reciprocal altruism *wholly* replaces altruism, the reality of the moral sphere of Faces is denied). In these influential paradigms, the moral reality at the root of all ethical conviction, agape, is elided.

Rehabilitating in all its wonder and power the moral reality of agape is essential, but it leads us onto dangerous terrain. For on this terrain one deals with subjective convictions, moral passions, the limitations of human reasoning, and, to put it mildly, fallible people. Notably, much of what I criticize as the scientism of modern philosophy and science, including most especially the emphasis upon dispassionate, objective reflection in ethics, began as an understandable and contextually legitimate reaction to ethical and religious extremism in Europe in the sixteenth and seventeenth centuries (including the torture and killing of "heretics," the Index, and the Inquisition). It is important to recall past mistakes and explicitly to name such dangers when they lurk in the shadows in order to guard against them. Christians like myself must acknowledge the shameful and cruel behavior of our forebears, and acknowledge that we must remain on continual guard against a repeat of such horrible offenses. On the other hand, in the face of what has become for many modern Western intellectuals an irrational allergy to religion, it is important to note that we no longer live in an age where the only societal dangers flow from religious or ethical extremism.

For instance, despite the continuing popularity of rhetoric blaming religion for warfare, the wars the United States has been involved in over roughly the last century—i.e., the Spanish-American War, the US-Filipino

---

1. See further on this point Greenway, "Peter Singer, Emmanuel Levinas, Christian Agape, and the Spiritual Heart of Animal Liberation."

war, World War I, World War II, the Korean War, the Vietnam War, the first and second Gulf Wars, the war in Afghanistan—have been rooted in disputes over territory, natural resources, and economic power/trade policy, not points of religious doctrine (while in some cases religion is obviously playing a motivating role, especially vis-à-vis popular opinion, even in such instances it is critical to tease out the significance of other factors). So while an aggressive modern turn to dispassionate, objective reason may once have been to a limited degree contextually justified, that contextual justification no longer holds in the West. This most certainly does not amount to dismissing concern over religious or ethical extremism, which is the focus of my next chapter.

What is now more significant is the way in which the modern emphasis upon dispassionate, objective reason has encouraged systemic denial of the sphere of moral reality generally. When this dynamic is combined with a focus upon ethical quandaries it fosters a widespread sense that *all* ethics is epiphenomenal (i.e., wholly a sociocultural product) and relativistic. That is ethically dangerous because it retards the social force of moral reality and its ethical implications even where there is no real ethical debate.

A general background conviction that all ethics is relative can create a social context in which the forces of greed, selfishness, neglect, and even exploitation can be freed of societal censure and restraint. The unleashing of these dynamics can kill or oppress as surely as wars (and one may indeed be able to connect the dots between the unleashing of such dynamics and many twenty- and twenty-first-century wars). Thus it is critical to counter the modern and postmodern eliding of primordial, moral reality. For not only is such denial simply inaccurate, the wholesale eliding of moral reality is itself a dangerous, immoral extremism that is increasingly serving as an ideological bulwark for an age of unbridled greed and exploitation (and such dynamics may fuel reactionary religious ideologies—contrary to a long-standing, widely held opinion of intellectual elites, the best alternative to extremist faith and/or ethical relativism may not be the wholesale rejection/denial of faith and moral reality, but reasonable faith and reasonable affirmation of moral reality).

In sum, classic modern Western philosophical ideals demand we appeal only to dispassionate theoretical foundations that cannot explain or stimulate ethical motivational energy, for they are inaccurate with regard to the source and character of ethical conviction. Modern philosophy and ethics achieved its most immediate and urgent goals by insisting upon

PART THREE: BEYOND OBJECTIVITY, RELATIVISM, AND EXTREMISM

dispassionate, objective, and logically indubitable foundations. Modern ethical theory was, thankfully, effective in de-legitimating much religious extremism. The scientific demand for objective ethical theory, however, ended up eliding the sphere of the moral altogether, and unintentionally helped lead us to the devastating moral lacunae that I (following Levinas) am here attempting to name and address.

Significantly, what actually and rightly motivated modern Western ethical theorists' opposition to religious extremism was not fidelity to an objective principle or rule, but a moral concern over awful violations of Faces. Most modern ethical theorists were rightly motivated by *moral* horror over religious extremism and violence and by *moral* passion for justice. But their wholesale rejection of the moral dimension of reality, a rejection intrinsic to the demand for objective, dispassionate reasoning, rendered modern theorists incapable of articulating the moral source of their own ethical convictions (the source, for instance, of their conviction that religious extremism is ethically wrong). That is, ethicists who in recent centuries have insisted upon appeals to objective, dispassionate first principles unwittingly elide at a conceptual level the very moral passions that energize their own ethical efforts.[2]

Although I am criticizing the modern Western eliding of the moral sphere, then, my argument is friendly to the actual ethical convictions of most modern ethicists and remains wholly appreciative of their rigorous analyses. I seek only to counter the eliding of agape and the scientific demand for dispassionate, objective, and logically indubitable ethical foundations. The trick is to rehabilitate primordial, moral, having been seized while avoiding both ethical relativism (the balance of this chapter) and ethical/religious extremism (next chapter). I begin by detailing a distinction between having been seized by love for Faces (i.e., agape, moral reality) and ethical conviction.

---

2. A most famous case would be that of Michel Foucault. Foucault's work has been celebrated because of its moral resonance, in particular, because it awakened readers to previously marginalized Faces. Foucault, however, remained faithful to the strictures of modern Western ratiocination, and always insisted that his work was only descriptive. This public commitment to modern principles of ratiocination kept Foucault from articulating fully and clearly the moral dynamics of his own work (a similar point could be developed vis-à-vis John Rawls and Peter Singer, among many others).

Against Ethical Relativism

AGAPE AND ETHICAL CONVICTION

In line with rehabilitation of the moral, and contrary to modern dreams and the Western philosophical mainstream, it has become evident that carefully reasoned ethical convictions are not ultimately derived from reason. That is, careful ethical reasoning alone does not produce ethical conviction. Nor is ethical conviction at root something you choose. You might choose not to be ethical (e.g., you may choose to do something out of self-interest even when you realize it is unethical), or you might choose to ignore or deny having been seized by love (i.e., you can harden your heart), but you do not *choose* to be seized by love for a Face. For example, the sobbing, bloodied child turns from the scene of the crime and the bodies of his parents and runs to you—you do not in that moment *choose* to be seized by the Face of that child. Careful ethical reasoning articulates ethical convictions. The ultimate motivational source of ethical convictions, however, is not any reasoning, but agape. That is, above and before all, ethical convictions are not a product of reason alone. Ethical convictions are a product of reason taken together with a more primordial having been seized by love for one or more Faces.

My position is not dismissive of reason. While reason alone is not the source of ethical conviction, I affirm that careful ethical reasoning is absolutely crucial to formulation and assessment of ethical convictions. In evaluating our loves and adjudicating among them in a world where they often conflict, there is need for careful and precise reasoning about ethical convictions. Reason can also help us to identify prejudices. We should always remember that our ethical convictions are not infallible. The immediate point here, however, is that reason is not the sole or primordial source of ethical convictions. Reason is what is essential if we are to understand and extrapolate rightly from pre-reflective, having been seized (moral reality).

The critical distinctions here are among *agape* (which is pre-reflective), *ethical judgment* (which involves reasoning), and *ethical convictions* (ethical judgments you hold with reasonable surety). Notably, when you attempt to describe the moral reality of having been seized by love for some Face, especially when you try to describe moments of intense joy, love, peace, pain, or horror, you run up against a source of the classic spiritual vocabulary of the indescribable, the infinite, the ineffable, or the sacred. For the attempt to describe fully the reality of having been seized by love for a Face always falls short. The very act of stepping out of the moment, reflecting upon it, and choosing appropriate words to describe or gesture toward it, that is, the very act of *thinking* immediately and decisively distances you from the primordial reality of having been seized.

After having been seized, upon reflection, as you strive for adequate words, you realize that however faithfully you gesture towards it, the immediate reality you want to share with others remains always to some degree beyond reach. The most articulate and moving poems, the most stirring music, the most evocative paintings about loves, joys, sorrows, and horrors (e.g., Edvard Munch's "The Scream," Pablo Picasso's "Guernica") all fall short of capturing the full reality to which they profoundly testify. The full reality of the love, joy, or sorrow by which one is seized is ultimately indescribable, ineffable.

The purity and immediacy of the primordial having been seized (of moral reality) is compromised and lost the instant one thinks *anything*. In the sheer, immediate intensity of the moment you do not think "moral," "good," "love," "seal," or "sapling." Such thinking, such concepts, may be virtually simultaneous with the primordial having been seized, but they are not equally primordial, for they are not themselves the having been seized. They are our immediate thinking of it.

To be sure, you cannot in any way name, understand, or choose to act without thinking, without some understanding, some reasoning. There is no possibility of merely and continually inhabiting having been seized by love for Faces. You immediately and quite rightly think, name, reflect, and act. But having been seized remains primordial, ineffable, and sacred. Your immediate *thinking* accompanies the moral, then, but it is not equally primordial. Sound ethical convictions are the result of having been seized by love plus the immediate, often fragmentary thinking (*"oh no, no, no!" "oh yes, thanks be, thanks be, thanks be," "Stevie!" "Anna!"*), plus also disciplined and complex reflection upon the meaning and implications of our having been seized by many Faces in diverse and sometimes torturously complicated contexts—and on this last score we quickly find ourselves in debt to the rigorous analyses of modern ethics.

When you are seized by love for some Face, then, you are seized *morally*, absolutely, pre-reflection, before the possibility of question or doubt. *Ethical convictions*, by contrast, are the products not only of having been seized (moral reality) but *also* of ethical reasoning (i.e., of culturally conditioned, contingent, fallible human reasoning). That is, our ethical convictions are sustained not merely by having been seized by love for a variety of Faces, but also by interpretations of the significance and meaningfulness of having been seized in specific historical contexts and by conclusions about how we should adjudicate among and prioritize Faces.

In contrast to the purity and the immediate, subjective indubitableness of your primordial, moral, having been seized by any particular Face, then, your *ethical convictions* are subject to the prejudices and limitations of language, culture, reasoning ability, and personal character. Ethical convictions, moreover, are immediately caught up in all the contradictory demands and needs of a multitude of Faces. For all Faces are bound up together in the conflicted realities of life. The pre-reflective, subjective indubitableness that is experienced from within the grip of primordial, moral, having been seized, therefore, should not be attached to the ethical ideas that appear as immediately as thought itself.

The significance of the distinction between having been seized by Faces (the moral) and *ethical* conviction is that it allows us to gesture to the wonder and power of moral reality while providing a basis for distinguishing surety from certainty. This distinction allows us to avoid ethical relativism, on the one hand (this chapter), and ethical extremism, on the other (next chapter). Let me now detail the reasonableness of ethical surety over and against widespread modern Western affirmation of ethical relativism.

SURETY NOT CERTAINTY:
THE ILLUSION OF ETHICAL RELATIVISM

The modern ethical ideal of objective certainty is not only inaccurate but also dangerous because it can lead to denial of agape (i.e., the moral reality of having been seized by love for Faces), and that makes proclamation of ethical relativism not only amoral but immoral. Unfortunately, those who are willfully immoral can exploit modernity's inability to articulate its moral roots and its inability to meet its own demand for objective, logically indubitable, and dispassionate ethical foundations. In particular, they can exploit those inabilities in order to abrogate moral concerns and responsibilities altogether. This becomes most pronounced when the inherent weakness of the modern ethical ideal, namely, the impossibility of establishing objective and certain first principles in ethics, is used to undercut the legitimacy and authority of any ethical pronouncement whatsoever. Then we hear supposedly reasonable proclamations of ethical relativism.

The proclamation of ethical relativism is wholly dependent upon what is now conceded to be an impossible demand for dispassionate, objective foundations, and it tends to weaken the force of any ethical appeal. For instance, the sense that all ethical conviction is relativistic and wholly the result of social and physical conditioning is dangerous insofar as it can leave an amoral and anemic appeal to enlightened self-interest (e.g., social contract theory) as the only brake against wholesale social and economic Darwinism (which arguably is, *de facto*, the brutal, ruling background cosmology of the modern West and, increasingly, of a transnational economic elite).

Rehabilitation of morality is essential to furthering the possibility that we might cultivate as fully as possible not simply a materially secure and scientifically advanced civilization, but a *good* civilization (and it is not at all clear that in the long run a civilization that is not morally awake and striving for the good can be secure). This should not be read as a call for a political naivety that could easily be crushed by those bent on exploitation and/or oppression. This is a call to remain true to ethical ideals while remaining realistic about the realities of worldly powers. This is a call for nations to strive to be both great *and* good.

Although the threat of prejudice and self-interest and the inability to gain objective certainty with regard to many ethical convictions should make us cautious, these considerations do not legitimate assertion of ethical relativity. Unfortunately, the modern obsession with certainty and the consequent focus in modern ethics upon ethical quandaries has often unjustifiably undercut confidence in the reality of the moral and undercut confidence in ethical convictions shared by diverse peoples for millennia. Those obsessed with certain foundations miss the significance and even forget the reality of that vast array of ethical convictions with regard to which surety is legitimately and powerful grounded by profound and overwhelming having been seized by love for Faces *in combination with* ethical consensus that is historically deep and culturally diverse.[3]

For instance, it is easy to take university courses in ethics which focus exclusively upon cases where there is profound ethical ambiguity, and in such contexts it is easy for the casual thinker to get the impression that since ethical decision-making with regard to quandary cases is unsettled, *all* ethics must be likewise unsettled. Indeed, it is not unusual to hear otherwise insightful students affirm that modern reason leads us inexorably to

---

3. The influence of C. S. Pierce and William James is manifest when I talk of "surety" and the lack of "any real doubt" instead of acceding to the modern demand for "certainty" (i.e., "certainty" as understood in the wake of the classic Cartesian epistemological definition of certainty in terms of *logical* indubitableness).

Against Ethical Relativism

acknowledge ethical relativity. It is not insignificant that virtually no one who affirms ethical relativity really believes what they are saying. Virtually no one believes, for instance, that there is ethical relativity involved in the judgment that it is good to make children giggle and evil to torture them for amusement.

Now, again, evidently there are some people who actually do see such unquestionably horrible acts as real-life options. For instance, there evidently are people who could hear real-life descriptions of torture, rape, and murder without feeling a moral twinge (or, worse, who actually experience pleasure). But such people are not ethical counterexamples, and if any act on their belief that torturing little boys and girls is good fun, then people should do whatever is immediately necessary to stop them from engaging in that activity, and after that they should secure them in a mental institution or a jail. You may feel bad for and even try to help such people. Indeed, love for all others should extend to those who do evil. But in such cases we should not lose any sleep over our ethical judgments or entertain any real doubt about whether or not our ethical convictions are justified.

If, for instance, you find yourself in an ethically clear-cut situation in which you must act coercively (perhaps you are a police officer) in order to protect some innocent from being wounded or killed, then you should act with the degree of violence necessary to protect the innocent from harm. Insofar as you are forced to harm someone, then, since you love even enemies (i.e., because you are awake to all Faces), you will mourn the coercion and make it as minimal as possible, but you will realize that you are caught in a situation where to act coercively is less evil than not to act at all. Your feelings, then, will rightly be conflicted. There may well be ethical debates over the degree of coercion that is justified in given situations but, and this is the point here, there is no good reason to wonder if perhaps some psychopath is right after all about the gratuitous torture of toddlers.[4] There is no reason in such contexts to affirm or worry over ethical relativism.

Despite all the affirmations of ethical relativism, there are a multitude of ethical convictions that are so fundamental, so little in doubt, so widely affirmed across cultures and across centuries, that there is no basis whatsoever for entertaining real doubt about them. One can claim culturally diverse, historically deep intersubjectively substantiated surety about

---

4. To speak very technically for a moment, this is why Levinas contends that "ethics" in contrast to "epistemology" is "first philosophy" (remember that what Levinas means by ethics in this sense I am calling the moral, the reality of having been seized by love).

PART THREE: BEYOND OBJECTIVITY, RELATIVISM, AND EXTREMISM

a multitude of ethical convictions that provide a sure basis for judging people's character (e.g., greed is not good, she is greedy) and, in numerous cases, even for institutionalizing them (e.g., adults having sexual relations with children is not good, he has engaged in pedophilia, he should be institutionalized). That is, congruence in the collective wisdom of multiple peoples across cultures and history, all of whom have been awakened to the same moral reality, quite reasonably adds overwhelming though not absolute weight to ethical convictions (I say "not absolute" because prejudices too can be carried by traditions; I address the threat of such systemic distortions in detail below).[5]

>   5. Speaking technically, let me stress I am indebted to Hans-Georg Gadamer, and most especially his famous rehabilitation of tradition and authority in *Truth and Method*, when I appeal not only to the immediate authority of one's own primordial, moral, having been seized, but also and essentially to the reasonableness of affirming ethical convictions that are also shared across cultures and across centuries. This is meant to invoke a very important aspect of Gadamer's "classical example," with its affirmation of the wisdom, though not the infallibility, of judgments that prove themselves by virtue of their elevation and continuing relevance over time within a tradition, a wisdom reasonably accorded even greater weight vis-à-vis judgments that have endured not only within one tradition, but that have long been shared by multiple traditions and cultures. My invocation of critical theory, inspired above all by the work of Jürgen Habermas, brings into play an active caution and guard against the susceptibility of Gadamer's appeal to the classical to systemic distortions that may be unconsciously carried by a tradition. In setting Gadamer's (the classical example) and Habermas's (suspicion of systemic distortions) two incommensurable trajectories of thought in sustained tension I am following Paul Ricoeur (see especially "The Task of Hermeneutics" and "Hermeneutics and the Critique of Ideology," both in *Hermeneutics and the Social Sciences*). Notably, to the degree critical theory has been captured by language-dependent emphases upon communicative competence (as in Habermas), critical theory itself has tended to reinforce a systemic distortion that disallows regard for creatures who lack advanced linguistic capacity. In addition, Gadamer's appeal to the classical example remains caught within the logic of Levinas's "Same" in a fashion that creates palpable dissonance when one reads *Truth and Method* (i.e., Gadamer manifests a conviction over the reality of moral truth that he can never quite accommodate in his theory). To Gadamer's appeal to the classical example, then, I am adding Levinasian alterity and, most especially, the moral revelation embedded within our having been seized by love for the Faces of others. It is such encounters with Faces that play the critical theoretical role in my account that appeals to an ideal, utterly non-coercive speech community or to undistorted communicative reason play in Habermas's account (or, outside the bounds of critical theory, appeal to the "originary position" played in John Rawls's *A Theory of Justice*). I would want to suggest that an appeal to Faces has always secretly provided moral energy to critical theory. That is, what critical theorists have really been about (even, for instance, Foucault, who would have denied it) has been the unveiling of systemic distortions that wound the Faces of others. The moral force of their critiques, I submit, results from their effective but under-theorized unveiling of the Faces of marginalized faces. Habermas makes this

Against Ethical Relativism

With regard to morals and ethics, then, we are not faced with a choice between either "objective and certain" or "relativistic." The modern demand for certainty and objectivity in the realm of morality and ethics was an understandable overreaction to the very real dangers and devastatingly realized potentials of religious extremism. But modern Western intellectuals largely rebounded to the opposite and equally dangerous extreme of eliding morality and conceding ethical relativism. In this vein, purportedly postmodern proclamations of "ethical relativism" presume the modern either/or between objective certainty and relativity and, recognizing the impossibility of reaching certain and objective ethical judgments, default to "relativism." We should reject the either/or. Objective certainty in the modern Cartesian sense is indeed beyond human reach, but our confidence should not be controlled by a demand for indubitable knowledge. Theoretical certainty is beyond reach, but vis-à-vis a vast array of judgments (e.g., torture of toddlers for fun is evil) there is no reason for any real doubt.[6]

While I make no claims to objectivity or certainty, then, my argument is wholly rational and spiritually accurate. Our surety (not certainty, but no real or reasonable doubt) with regard to a host of ethical judgments is justifiably strong. In contrast to a devastating misstep by some influential streams of modern ethical theory, at the core of this argument is an appeal to the moral force of having been seized by love for every Face. Such an appeal is not legitimate in areas like mathematics, physics, or chemistry, but it is an essential aspect of any ethical argument. What would be unreasonable would be to insist that ethics restrict itself to the boundaries of rationality appropriate to the natural or social sciences.

---

unwitting, self-deceiving dynamic visible in *The Philosophical Discourse of Modernity*. But Habermas, like Gadamer, remains caught within modern Western conceptual parameters, and so he remains cut off from the possibility of affirming moral realism in the classic, Levinasian sense.

6. Technical note on politics and the possibilities for a post-secular state: no theory of justice in the modern sense is possible and a sheer political liberalism (e.g., the later work of John Rawls), while very promising, will remain radically incomplete insofar as it does not articulate the reality and moral force of agape, which is at the heart of every particular ethical conviction. The idea of "overlapping consensus" that Rawls developed in *Political Liberalism* has considerable potential for reconstituting a "public" sphere in the wake of the collapse of the conceptual foundations of the modern public/private split and the recognition that, for instance, "secular humanist," "liberal atheism," and so forth, name traditioned and essentially religious rationalities (i.e., rationalities that presume distinct metaphysics). Notably, in *Political Liberalism* Rawls continues to perpetuate the modern Western mistake of eliding the moral. Rawls's position would be strengthened if it were supplemented by Levinas's moral realism.

Part Three: Beyond Objectivity, Relativism, and Extremism

We can wholly reasonably say "no," then, to the quintessentially modern demand for dispassionate, objective, logically indubitable ethical argument and still quite reasonably avoid any descent into ethical relativism. We can wholly reasonably affirm that vast array of ethical convictions with regard to which surety is legitimately and powerfully grounded by profound and overwhelming having been seized by love for Faces *in combination with* ethical consensus that is historically deep and culturally diverse. Thus—the point of this chapter—we can wholly reasonably reject ethical relativism.

Awakening, Moral Realism, Moral Injury: Three Brief Student Stories about Killing Animals

I once had a student whose father was a famous, professional, "master" hunter. He became so skilled that he moved from rifle, to bow and arrow, to knife. To hunt with a knife, my student explained to me, one has to know the animal and its habits and habitat intimately. Her father never stopped loving the hunt. He loved melting into the habitat, living intimately with the animal, anticipating its moves, sensing what it sensed. But over time, she told me, especially in the wake of the terrible intimacy and honesty of the knife, he came to hate the kill.

* * * * *

One of my students was from Korea. According to her, a classic Korean custom required that before one killed any animal one had to look it straight in the face and meet its gaze, looking deeply into its eyes. In this way, she said, one only killed after owning fully the magnitude of what one was about to do. She did not use Levinasian jargon, but clearly this custom was meant to ensure that whoever was going to kill had seen the Face of the creature, had discerned the moral horror of the killing, had fully appreciated what they were about to do to another, and to themselves.[7]

---

[7]. Another Korean student I had a few years later had never heard of this custom so, while there is no reason to doubt the word of the first student, I am not sure if the custom was widespread. This, "do . . . to themselves" is an instance of what is named vis-à-vis soldiers as "moral injury" (I discuss moral injury below).

Against Ethical Relativism

* * * * *

Another of my students came from a proud military family in the States (she went on to become an Army chaplain who served in Iraq). She told me that her father and a cousin, both Vietnam vets, both of whom fought drug addiction, had been assigned to the kill room in the cattle processing plant where they worked. In the kill room workers kill a cow every few minutes. When they were given their assignment, their supervisor explained to her father and cousin the reason why they were selected for that brutal job: it was because of their backgrounds, they were told, because they were already well accustomed to death and killing. In a cruel and backhanded way that rationale bore testimony to the Faces of the cows, and signaled that the infliction of moral injury upon her father and cousin—pain from being turned into serial killers, pain from causing and witnessing terror and death—was far from over.

Chapter 8

Against Ethical Extremism

Reasonable and proportionate ethical convictions

I am seeking to rehabilitate the moral sphere, to tear down a conceptual wall that has blinded us to a multitude of Faces. I am seeking to rehabilitate a severely damaged but still widely felt sense for the sacredness of all life. In that sense my quest is profoundly spiritual and profoundly moral, and it addresses the empowering heart of all ethical conviction. At the same time, the move into the realm of moral passion, the affirming and invoking of the reality of having been seized by love for all Faces, and the rejection of the modern demand for dispassionate, objective, logically certain foundations: all of these can seem to bring into play dangerous energies conducive to extremism and violence.

To the contrary, however, it is important to stress first and last that the realm of moral passion is not dangerous. For the realm of the moral is not the realm of selfishness, greed, cowardice, envy, spite, lust, pride, or hatred; it is the realm of agape. It is precisely that realm that most profoundly moves people beyond self-interest to compassion, the realm of having been seized by love for all Faces.

This point can seem counterintuitive to modern Westerners because modern thought successfully curbed violent excesses of religious extremism through appeal to objective and dispassionate reasoning, and so it can seem

Against Ethical Extremism

to modern Westerners that to undo this appeal is to open the floodgates to extremism. The modern ideal of objective and dispassionate reasoning was motivated by good moral impulses and was very effective. As argued above, however, the modern ideal is unsatisfactory because it is inaccurate and, in the long run, dangerous to morality and ethics. It is inaccurate because it is unable to articulate the moral roots of ethical conviction. It is dangerous because it leads to the conceptual eliding of the moral realm altogether and empowers declarations of ethical relativism.

Fortunately, as is now clear, the impossibility of grounding ethics upon objective and dispassionate reasoning does not entail a denial of moral realism, and it does not entail ethical relativism. Given the awful history of and enduring damage resulting from ethical and religious extremism, however, it is necessary to explain in detail why rehabilitating the moral passion (i.e., the having been seized) in ethical conviction does not empower ethical or religious extremism. The points I will now briefly delineate have been implicit throughout my argument. That is, I have already invoked criteria that allow reasonable discernment of appropriate degrees of humility or confidence vis-à-vis diverse ethical convictions, and that allow delineation of degrees of coercion or violence appropriate to diverse situations.

For instance, as explained above, the disintegration of the modern ethical ideal of establishing all ethical judgments upon the basis of objective and dispassionate reasoning does not reduce us to relativism, and it does not leave us defenseless against sheer advocacy of personal opinion. Radical subjectivity and personal idiosyncrasy are preempted by the distinction between having been seized (moral reality) and ethical conviction. This distinction clearly distinguishes the individual, subjective experience of pre-reflective absoluteness that attends having been seized by love for a Face, from the potential prejudices or errors in judgment that may afflict ethical convictions.

A multitude of ethical convictions are quite reasonably *sure* (if not certain in the modern sense). But appeal to surety is grounded not only in the moral, that is, in having been seized, but also in intersubjective confirmation. There is no good reason to harbor any real doubts about humanity's most profound and widely shared ethical convictions.

This appeal to the wisdom of communities, that is, to interculturally wide and historically deep intersubjective verification, fulfills the first aspect of the critical role that the appeal to "objectivity" played in modern Western ethical theory. For it requires everyone to look beyond their

Part Three: Beyond Objectivity, Relativism, and Extremism

personal and also their own community's perspectives and convictions, and simultaneously provides a reasonable basis for recognizing and critiquing idiosyncratic or narrowly shared ethical convictions.[1] Moreover, insofar as self-interest is utterly overwhelmed by the responsibility and compassion of agape, the appeal to Faces effectively and profoundly displaces the prejudicial influence of self-interest. Notably, precisely such neutralization of the biases of self-interest was the second aspect of the critical role that the appeal to objectivity played in the modern ideal.[2]

At the same time, at the level of moral reality, the modern demand that we be "dispassionate" is replaced with invocation of the moral reality of agape. The demand for dispassion was modernity's important and admirable brake against the likes of disgust, hatred, bitterness, or envy that so awfully fueled and fuels extremist violence. In place of "dispassion," the appeal to a primordial responsiveness, to response-ability and responsibility, to having been seized by love for the Faces of all others—even saplings, even enemies—is the Levinasian brake against extremist violence.

Accordingly, this argument has emphasized the role of intersubjective verification, respect for collective and historical wisdom, and an absolutely fundamental sensitivity to every Face, even the Faces of saplings and enemies. All these are critical to a rehabilitation of moral reality that is, first and foremost, spiritually accurate, and that also quite reasonably avoids the dual dangers of ethical relativism and ethical extremism. Quite reasonably, then, we can without any real doubts distinguish ethical convictions that are very sure from those that are less so (e.g., very sure regarding gratuitous killing, less sure regarding a host of familiar quandary cases). All this describes moral and ethical dynamics that are wholly ordinary and familiar.

The appeal to degrees of communal, historic, and cross-cultural affirmation allows us to draw reasonable distinctions among central and more peripheral ethical convictions. In the end, we quite reasonably own with utmost confidence, with surety (but not certainty), ethical convictions that are, first, most intimately connected to having been seized by love for the Faces of others *and*, second, that have been most fully shared by generation upon generation of moral beings throughout history and across civilizations.

1. Stipulating a need for both interculturally wide and historically deep inter-subjective verification should mitigate both relativistic individualist and group-think/group-interest communitarian extremes.

2. For example, the role of Rawls's imaginary "original position" or Habermas's imaginary "ideal speech community."

Against Ethical Extremism

This also provides general parameters for discerning levels of violence or coercion appropriate to various ethical convictions. Generally, the more sure an ethical conviction, the more coercion or violence is appropriate to prevent its violation. In every case, however, unfailing sensitivity to the Face of the perpetrator, love even for enemies, dictates actions towards perpetrators (e.g., the need to resort to violence is always awful) and modulates the degree of the violence (i.e., we resort to violence only when absolutely necessary and only to the minimal degree required). By contrast, we encounter extremism when the violence is disproportionate to the surety or exceeds what is minimally required to preserve good or to prevent evil, or when the Faces of others are elided (e.g., when we do not love our enemy).

Consider this example of non-extremist, lethal violence. I had a student who had been a police officer. One day he found himself the lead officer, gun drawn, in a tense standoff with a violent criminal who was desperate, irrational, and most likely high on drugs. The man, cornered by officers, was holding up a brick in one hand and cradled a human baby with his opposite arm. The man was yelling that he was going to kill the baby with the brick. When he moved to club the baby my student shot him. The man was killed, the baby saved. In this case there is high surety with regard to the pertinent ethical convictions and, even though the violence was deadly, it was the least violent option available in the circumstance.

It is important to specify that violence toward any Face is always awful—even when the violence is unquestionably justified (e.g., violent actions soldiers or police officers may take). That is, even when the violence is the right action it is never in and of itself a good action. It may be the best and only action that an ethical person can take, but that will nonetheless be the case only because one has been forced to choose among morally bad alternatives. The violence may be the right action insofar as it is the least bad alternative and so ethically required, but that does not make it a good action. Sometimes the best ethical alternative is morally bad.

My student still had to deal with the fact that, though justified, he had looked that man "in the eye," that is, in the Face, and killed him. Killing is never morally good. In that sense, in taking the right ethical action my student wounded *himself*, for he was put into a context within which he had to choose among bad options, and in this case the best option involved killing another person. In this sense, police officers or soldiers who act ethically (not just legally, but ethically) *wound themselves* when they are forced by circumstance to act violently against others (this is a moral injury to keep in mind when counseling ethical persons who have found themselves compelled to violate Faces). In sum, despite the lethal violence, and because my student did see the Face of the man he killed, this is not a case of extremist violence.

Could this example regarding the police officer and a baby be extrapolated and applied to a person who kills a doctor who performs abortions? Certainly not—no matter your ethical convictions regarding abortion. In the first place, and setting aside the very significant fact that the police officer is fulfilling officially sanctioned duties and so setting aside as well the need to justify anarchic actions, even if it were a particular fetus that was being defended, with respect to the question of abortion there is widespread disagreement among people who are otherwise reasonable and of good character, so no one can claim sufficient intersubjective confirmation, sufficient surety with regard to the issue of abortion to justify killing someone who performs abortions.

Second, with regard to abortion there are non-violent, political means that can be used in opposition, thus the resort to violence is not necessitated. The killing of a doctor who performs abortions, then, would be an act of extremism because, among other factors, it is disproportionate to warranted ethical surety and is, with regard to the goal of ending the practice of abortion, not minimally violent (this reasoning should be affirmed both by those who are "pro-choice" and by those who are "pro-life"). Similar reasoning should also lead us to conclude that the actions of an animal rights advocate who killed someone because they conducted experiments upon animals should likewise be condemned as extremist (I am not aware of any incidents where this has actually happened, but it is worth noting in principle).

Even with these relatively clear-cut examples there are many significant complexities that could be explored, and the examples could easily be tweaked to make the ethical dilemmas more pronounced, but all such would take us into the realm of ethics proper, which is not now our task (I take this up in part four). Nevertheless, these examples should suffice to make clear our general ability in principle to delineate as clearly as is possible the continuum from justified to unjustified (i.e., extremist) action.

In sum, we quite reasonably enjoy surety regarding ethical convictions that are both intimately connected to having been seized by love for the Faces of others and that are also shared by generation upon generation of moral beings throughout history and across civilizations. The more there

Against Ethical Extremism

is surety about an ethical conviction (e.g., it is wrong to kill a baby with a brick), the more coercion or violence is appropriate to prevent its violation. But we never forget the Face of the perpetrator. Thus even in clear-cut cases we resort to violence only when absolutely necessary, only to the minimal degree required, and always with remorse over the necessity of violence. To act coercively to a degree not necessary and/or unwarranted by ethical surety, or ever to fail to see the Face of any other would be to participate in extremist violence.

Inescapable complexities

Good and wise people wholly awakened to agape will always confront significant ethical ambiguity over right action amidst the complexities of our conflicted world. Many real-world dilemmas require adjudication among incommensurable claims from diverse Faces, such that any choice made will compromise fidelity to some Face(s), and this often in contexts in which the most ethical path is not obvious. Life is filled with substantial regions of moral ambiguity (for instance, regarding varieties of euthanasia or genetic engineering). In these regions of ambiguity, the moral, that is, having been seized by love for the Faces of others, typically provides no direct ethical guidance. Nor does the moral provide direct ethical guidance on occasions when we find ourselves seized by different Faces that inform diverse ethical convictions in mutual conflict.

For instance, in questions of euthanasia, the conviction that it is wrong to kill is typically in conflict with a conviction that it is good to hasten an end to terminal physical agony. Both may even be sympathetic, ethical reactions to the same Face (e.g., the mortally wounded soldier, blown apart by the land mine deep in the jungle, screams for his buddy to kill him in order to end his suffering quickly). Realism about wrenching ethical quandaries in which the stakes are tremendous and the ethics ambiguous should generate proportionate humility. Just as with regard to many ethical judgments there is no reason for doubt, with many other ethical judgments there is no reason for confidence.

My defense of moral realism, then, in no way facilitates any claim to definitive answers with regard to the many ethical quandary cases that divide awakened people of good will and character. Indeed, most concrete ethical debates will remain almost wholly unchanged by affirmation of the moral reality unveiled in having been seized by love for the Faces of all creatures. No one can provide a magical shortcut to surety over answers to legitimate ethical quandaries. Carefully reasoned ethical argument is essential if one is to choose as wisely as possible when the best path is not clear and every option involves compromise.

What distinguishes my neo-Levinasian approach from predominant modern Western theoretical approaches is the realization that ethical convictions are the product not primordially of reason, but primordially of agape. At the root of and so permeating all ethics there is no principle or end (e.g., the principle of autonomy, or "the greatest good for the greatest number"). Nor is there some absolute and/or cleanly delineated set of ethical givens or rational foundation (e.g., no categorical imperative, original position, sphere of undistorted communicative reason). At the foundation of and so permeating all ethics is primordial having been seized by love for the Faces of all creatures, that is, agape. This does not leave one with ethical relativity or ethical extremism, but with ethical convictions that can reasonably be placed along a continuum extending from more to less surety, and with a correlating method of adjudicating appropriate use of force.

An inescapable danger: systemic distortion

By this point the conservative (in the philosophical sense) cast of my approach is manifest. First, moral realities are as real as gravity. That is, to the degree that having been seized by love for all Faces is primordial, undeniable, and pre-intentional, then in its own nonphysical way the moral realm is as concrete and real, if not as irresistible, as the gravity that right now secures me to the floor. Second, the appeal to intersubjective confirmation, and in particular to the collective wisdom of communities across time and cultures is conservative (in a philosophical sense) insofar as it tends to privilege mainstream cultural norms. This is unavoidable but also potentially problematic insofar as mainstream norms may be biased against weaker or more marginal members of a community.

It is possible for systemic distortions (e.g., a sustained bias against women or against nonhuman creatures) to be sustained across centuries and to be common across cultures. Thus caution is needed with regard to continual susceptibility to the possibility not merely that anyone may be wrong in their ethical convictions, but that societies collectively and largely unwittingly can carry wholesale misunderstandings that cloak and/or betray moral reality. We may be mistaken even with regard to ethical

Against Ethical Extremism

convictions about which many people throughout history and across cultures entertained no real doubts.

The threat of systemic distortion does nothing to undo the collapse of modern appeals to dispassionate, objective knowledge. No matter how much we may wish it were not the case, there is simply no place outside of history and culture where we can turn to escape the threat of systemic distortion. The risk posed by difficult-to-discern systemic error is quite properly a source of real humility and caution with regard even to ethical convictions that are historically deep and culturally diverse—most especially as those ethical convictions may begin to appear to be in significant tension with primordial, moral, having been seized by love for the Faces of others. Since moral reality is as real as gravity, however, the inescapable risk of systemic error is reason for nothing more than humility. It is not a basis for ethical cynicism. In particular, there is no justification for allowing healthy realism about moral fallibility to legitimate a wholesale rejection of the reality of agape or of the reliability of humanity's most sure ethical convictions.

Notably, my argument includes a critique of two systemic distortions. First, I criticized scientistic rejection of moral reality. I argued that the rejection of the moral (in the classic, realist sense) is itself a product of systemic distortions that afflict preeminent forms of both modern and postmodern rationality. In seeking to unmask this distortion I made two moves. I appealed to having been seized by love for the Faces of others (i.e., agape), a moral reality to which the vast majority of people across cultures have testified for millennia. At the same time, I attempted to describe clearly and so make visible essential elements of the distortion (e.g., by distinguishing "science" from "scientism"). In sum, I attempted to describe and so to unmask and defang the conceptual dimensions of the distortion while simultaneously stimulating direct awakening to the moral reality the distortion elided.

I made the same twofold maneuver in response to a second systemic distortion, the eliding of the Faces of all nonhuman creatures. In this case, I used narrative in an attempt to provoke awakening to having been seized by love for nonhuman creatures. That was the wholly reasonable, moral/spiritual force of my appeal to the Faces of Kiki, the cricket at the airport, the whales trapped under ice, the seal trapped in the seashore tank, the orca, the maple sapling, and the deer killed by that wonderful Texan with his balloons and teddy bears. At the same time, I attempted to describe clearly and make visible essential elements of the distortion (e.g., by pointing out ways in which modern rationality relegated nonhuman creatures to the sphere of the machine). In sum, once again, I attempted to describe and so to unmask and defang the conceptual dimensions of the distortion while simultaneously stimulating direct awakening to the moral reality the distortion elided.

There is no dispassionate, objective, certain basis for ethics. There is no logical path leading to sure resolution of every ethical issue. Everyone is susceptible to understandable prejudices brought on by social conditioning, selfishness, ambition, and/or fear. Moreover, the threat of systemic distortion (i.e., unwitting prejudice, ideology) always looms over us. All this simply describes the character and vulnerability of moral reality and ethical convictions, and there is no long-term control or safety to be had in either denying moral reality or in denying the reality of these limitations. We need to guard against two dangerous and opposite positions: first, wholesale eliding of moral reality and a proclamation of ethical relativism (whether individualistic or communitarian), and second, reactionary denial of our inescapable susceptibility to error and false claims to ethical objectivity.

Fortunately, we need not be trapped by this extremist either/or (i.e., either relativity or certainty). We can quite reasonably enjoy surety with regard to our most profound occasions of having been seized by love for Faces and with regard to our most widely shared ethical convictions. It is reasonable to appeal to our primordial, moral, having been seized by love in our struggle to discern as reasonably as possible what is good and just. Using the criteria delineated above, we can reasonably adjudicate degrees of surety and appropriate use of force. At the same time, we are given reason to remain humble and appropriately open to criticism or new insight, aware that we may be deceived by systemic distortions. In sum, we can affirm moral passion without empowering ethical or religious extremism.

A COUNTER TO ETHICAL EXTREMISM: THE POWER OF FACES

Finally—true to my affirmation at the beginning of this chapter that this concern is of paramount importance—let me stress again that having been seized by love for the Faces of all creatures, including people, including crickets and saplings, including even enemies, is the most powerful brake against the historic and enduring dangers of ethical and religious prejudice

Against Ethical Extremism

and extremism. It is also our most powerful stimulus toward the good and the just. Agape, that is, having been seized by love for every Face, even the Faces of those who deny, inflict harm upon, and thereby make themselves the enemies of other Faces, is a reality that precludes extremist violence or fanatical devotion to a cause, doctrine, or principle, and is a reality that precludes unbridled devotion to self-interest.

What makes extremist violence not just illegitimate but literally unthinkable for those awake to the Faces of others is the fact that they do not desensitize themselves to the profound, having been seized by love for the Faces of *any* others, even enemies, thus even justified violence is painful and unwanted. Awakening to having been seized by love for all Faces is the ultimate and authentic source of all love, goodness, and justice. It is also an incredibly powerful brake against religious and ethical extremism and violence.

Chapter 9

All Life is Sacred

Faces: Morally Invaluable, Ethically Unequal

I have drawn a distinction between the moral and the ethical. In the transcending purity of having been seized by love for a Face, one is *morally* seized utterly and without qualification. Thus the moral is primordial, ineffable, prior to all reasoning. The ethical, by contrast, is distinguished from the moral precisely by virtue of being conceptual. *Ethics is thinking of and from the moral*, thus it benefits from but is susceptible to the contingencies of history, language, and reasoning. Because of this difference in kind there is no underlying calculus one can utilize to move precisely from the moral to the ethical. Nonetheless, while modern demands for dispassionate, objective conceptual foundations in ethics are unrealistic, and while there is no definite calculus one can develop in order to move from the moral to the ethical, the moral lies in fact at the root of the ethical, and one can articulate clearly and accurately the sometimes ambiguous but always critical influence of moral awakening for ethical conviction.

Any "ethical" not rooted in the moral is empty. Moreover, any such "ethical" is not merely amoral but immoral to the degree it participates in the eliding of Faces. The moral, that is, having been seized by love for the Faces of others, agape, lies at the root of all genuine ethics. However, because of the difference in kind between the moral and the ethical, because the moral is having been seized prior to all reasoning, and because, in particular, one is seized by love for each Face individually and absolutely, infinitely, apart from any categorization and comparative evaluation, the moral without the ethical lacks an ability to discern among Faces.[1]

The moral, then, is indebted to the ethical, beginning from the moment it is barely conceptualized, thought, or named (*"oh no, no, no!"* *"oh yes, thanks be, thanks be, thanks be,"* *"Stevie!"* *"Anna!"*) and enters into history. In itself the moral is helpless to name, compare, or choose among Faces, or to discriminate among possible actions in order to aid, defend, comfort, or bless Faces. One needs both the ethical and the moral, for *the ethical without the moral is empty* and *the moral without the ethical remains outside of thinking and history.*

The difference in kind between the moral and the ethical returns us to a classic ethical conundrum. To say one is seized by love for each Face individually and absolutely outside of history is to express in different words the classic moral and religious conviction that every human life, every soul, is of infinite value, is invaluable, holy, sacred. So—the classic conundrum—how can one legitimately make comparative ethical judgments when one is forced to discriminate among infinitely valuable Faces?

Notably, it is only as long as one remains within anthropocentric parameters (i.e., where to testify to the infinite value of every Face is simultaneously and solely to testify to the infinite value of every *human* life) that one faces this familiar conundrum. In the position defended here, the familiar conundrum is amplified. For not only is any imposition of anthropocentric parameters theoretically illicit because it surreptitiously imports historical, conceptual categories (e.g., "human") into the moral sphere, it is morally inaccurate because my analysis entails a strong affirmation that *morally* there is no basis for distinguishing between the Face of a human boy and the Face of a cat, worm, or sapling, for one is seized by love for each Face utterly, infinitely, and prior to all reflective discernment.

Nonetheless, if one were faced with a forced option between directing a train over a cat or over a boy, I would contend forcefully that one most certainly should direct the train to kill the cat. Indeed, the judgment that one should save the boy and cause the cat to be killed in such an instance is so sure that if someone declared that they would as soon cause the boy

---

1. When I use the term "infinite" I mean it in the Levinasian sense, which corresponds to the religious meaning of "eternal," which does not designate "unending time" but an "otherwise than being" outside of spatio-temporal categories in the natural/physical sense, an encounter with that which is overwhelming, ever opening, ever beyond one's grasp (cf. Greenway, *A Reasonable Belief*, 101–20).

as the cat to be killed, I would argue that they evidence a severe *ethical* incapacity (likewise if they simply refused to act, letting chance decide). My position, then, makes a strong *ethical* distinction between a boy and a cat, though this *ethical* distinction is incommensurable with primordial, *moral*, having been seized by love for the infinite and so incomparable value of the Faces of the boy *and* of the cat.

Because of the difference in kind between the moral and the ethical, and because moral realism and ethical reflection each possess essential and reasonable standing, there is no need to worry over the logical incommensurability between the moral and the ethical in and of itself. This incommensurability would have been a major stumbling block for mainstream modern thought, which presumed reality would be commensurate with human logic and so tended to equate "logically incommensurable" with "incoherent" (in a sense where "incoherence" equals "nonsense"). It is wholly reasonable, however, to embrace incommensurability if it is manifestly accurate to life, for it is unreasonable to gain wholesale commensurability at the cost of ignoring an overwhelmingly influential aspect of life. Therefore, both vocabularies that gesture beyond themselves toward the moral reality of agape (i.e., the reality of having been seized by love for Faces) and also vocabularies representing ethical realities and reasoning should be affirmed and engaged. One thereby gains poetic, spiritual accuracy and fullness at the expense of complete logical commensurability.

As the boy compared to the cat example illustrates, I need to develop some understanding of how people are to understand themselves in the face of these two incommensurable but critical aspects of life (i.e., the moral and the ethical). To this point, in response to modernity's eliding of moral reality, most of my argument has been dedicated to rehabilitating the moral and making clear the significance of having been seized by love (i.e., the significance of agape, of the moral) for ethical convictions. But, as the boy versus cat example makes clear, if I am to negotiate the incommensurability with completeness, I must also take care never to lose sight of the significance of ethical *judgment* for our ethical convictions. In straightforward cases, where the connection between having been seized by love for Faces and ethical conviction is direct and unproblematic, the reality and significance of ethical judgment for our ethical convictions is easy to miss (e.g., if the question is whether or not to save the cat by redirecting the train down a clear and safe track). But in cases where real life in real time forces one, *per impossibile*, to compare and choose among Faces, to "compare incomparables" (Levinas), the significance of ethical judgment becomes painfully apparent (the "painfully" is critical here, for it signals the enduring force of the moral).

Significantly, for many my moral equating of the Face of the boy and the Face of the cat will be scandalous. This makes manifest one major trajectory of resistance to my argument, namely, concern that I devalue human life. This trajectory of resistance is so powerful that I will defer discussing the relationship of ethical judgment and ethical conviction until the final part of the book, "Perfect Love in an Imperfect World: Agape Ethics." In the balance of this chapter, I will pause to name and address what I consider to be a quite understandable concern over moral equating (not ethical equating) of the Faces of humans, cats, and saplings.

The sanctity of life

When I contend that morally there is no basis for distinguishing the Face of a cat, worm, or sapling from the Face of a human boy, and when I go on to suggest in all seriousness that this creates an ethical challenge we need to address carefully, I can imagine even sympathetic readers worrying I have gone a bit overboard. I can imagine skeptical readers laughing out loud. I can imagine other readers reacting with fear and indignation. I feel some sympathy with each of these responses, but let me take a moment and briefly respond to what could well be the most morally sensitive response: the fear and indignation.

It is, of course, possible that the fear and indignation is simply a product of human pride, in which case it would not be a moral response at all. But the fear and indignation may also be a highly moral response. It is fear and indignation as a highly moral response that I want to respect and briefly address. In this moral vein, I would expect to find the fear and indignation to be profoundly if perhaps unconsciously linked to concern over a general devaluing of human life in modern Western culture. Notably, this concern is linked to a sense for the eliding of the moral realm in mainstream modern Western thought that my entire argument has been striving to unveil and counter.

I think people are rightly concerned that increasingly in modern Western societies even human life seems to be disposable. Human lives too have been turned into one among many commodities, commodities valued in terms of social power and economic status. In other words, the eliding of the moral realm, the eliding of all Faces, including human Faces, has led to a loss of the sense that every human life is invaluable. Many resist this devaluing of human life by stressing universal human rights (a predominant secular response), and/or by insisting that humans possess souls (a predominant theological response).

"Human rights" talk is clearly helpful rhetoric that has resulted in much good. Since the modern appeal to rights is based upon an appeal to a capacity for autonomy, however, it participates in modernity's eliding of the moral sphere at its very first step, for it understands the ultimate roots of ethics to lie in personal valuing of one's own capacity for self-determination, not in having been seized by love for the Faces of all faces (thus we find ourselves unable to escape the bounds of self-interest, enlightened or no). The modern appeal to souls, meanwhile, is inconsistent with mainstream modern rationality. Thus the appeal to souls has also been a nonstarter (with talk of "Faces" I am working to rehabilitate the essence of theological "soul" talk upon non-modern ground and, to speak technically, without invoking Cartesian-style, ontological/substance dualism).[2]

Moreover, the modern attempts to continue to distinguish humans absolutely and qualitatively—the attempts, really, to find some replacement for the classic affirmation that each human life is sacred, of infinite value, invaluable—all such modern attempts to generate or delineate this ethical conviction of an absolute qualitative distinction through sheer appeal to reason or concrete distinctions in capacities have failed. Worse yet, there are no doubt some who are eager (consciously or subconsciously) to invalidate all such attempts, some who would love to distinguish a hierarchy of value *among* humans, who would love to justify their privilege or, in some

---

2. Another major but less influential ethical trajectory that aims to resist modern Western devaluing of life is called "communitarianism." Just as is the case with the appeal to human rights and talk of souls, the communitarian approach accomplishes much that is good. But like the appeal to human rights it remains bound to intra-cultural *mores* and so fails to rehabilitate the moral sphere (in Levinasian terms, much communitarian thinking remains bound within the sphere of the Same). Consider, for instance, how Jeffrey Stout's unmitigated appeal to *Sittlichkeit* (notably, *sans Geist*) remains wholly within the sociocultural sphere (see Stout, *Democracy and Tradition*). Charles Taylor is a more promising figure in this regard. On the one hand, he details the historical sources of our most treasured *mores*, on the other hand he gestures to moral sources that transcend the historical (thereby gesturing beyond the confines of Gadamer's appeal to the classical example). Taylor's attempt to counter to what he calls a "leveling" in modern ethical reflection helped inspire my neo-Levinasian attempt to counter the eliding of the moral (see Taylor, *Sources of the Self*, and Greenway, "Charles Taylor on Affirmation, Mutilation, and Theism").

cases, their acts of oppression, by eliding the classic conviction that every human life is invaluable.

In other words, in a world in which everything not human has been reduced conceptually to commodity (to utility, to toaster ethics), the felt need to draw a bright moral line between humans and other creatures is palpable. This is especially the case because in fact predominant modern Western cultural imperatives drive us to value people too primarily as commodities, just as, with devastating results, it drives us to value nonhuman creatures as commodities. Thus beleaguered defenders of the sanctity of every human life, in an attempt establish a bulwark against oppressive and exploitative dynamics among people, have been backed into drawing a bright moral line between humans as a class (e.g., those who possess inalienable rights; those with souls) and everyone and everything else (including all other animals).

Obviously, those who are fighting this highly moral battle could perceive my erasure of the bright moral line as a mortal threat to our society's increasingly slender hold upon moral regard for the sanctity of human life. This could easily result in fear and indignation. To the degree that this, not pride, is the source of the fear and indignation, I think this is an understandable and admirable moral concern (indeed, as should be clear, I share this profound moral concern). Earlier I noted how even doctors at a Humane Society veterinary hospital referred to their cat and dog patients not by name but by model number. One increasingly hears similar complaints from humans (doctors, nurses, and patients alike) about the American medical industry's treatment of humans. We are one lesson. All creatures, nonhuman and human, are suffering from modernity's eliding of the moral dimension of reality.

Despite the admirable moral passion of those who are attempting to salvage something of a sense for the sanctity of human life by drawing a bright moral line between humans and all other creatures, however, no modern ethic has succeeded in setting humans apart morally as a class and in justifying the classic affirmation that every human life is invaluable, sacred, incomparable. This is hardly surprising, for predominant modern Western trajectories elide the moral sphere altogether.

Moreover, the idea that humans are set apart as a class is morally unstable insofar as we are not only seized by love for the Faces of humans, we are also seized by the Faces of cats, crickets, seals, orcas, and saplings. Thus we do not actually find humans to be absolutely distinguished morally as a class.³ So, affirmation of a bright moral line between humans and other creatures is not only theoretically untenable on modern premises, it requires morally sensitive people to deny many of their own most profound occasions of having been seized (i.e., their having been seized by love for the Faces of crickets, dogs, cats, horses, seals, and saplings).

The moral passion that leads many in the modern Western context to insist that humans are morally distinct as a class, then, is admirably focused upon resisting modernity's eliding of the moral sphere, but it is vulnerable and confused. Thus we can understand why modern Westerners with profound moral sensibilities could feel conflicted over my argument. On the one hand, their moral sensitivities would lead them to be profoundly loving and concerned in relation to nonhuman creatures, and so they would have been moved when my stories made manifest the Faces of nonhuman creatures. On the other hand, an admirable concern to resist the commodification of life has led many of them to attempt to draw a bright moral line by staking out humans as an infinitely valuable class of being—and that is a bright moral line my argument erases.

As is by this point clear, however, this bright moral line is in fact devastatingly fragile, for there is no moral, ethical, or philosophical justification for distinguishing humans morally as a class. It is not surprising, then, that the ideas that all are created equal and/or that each human life is of sacred value are exercising ever-decreasing sway in our culture. I am not only sympathetic to but also glad and affirming of those who defend the sanctity of life vis-à-vis humans. Their concern is rooted in sensitivity to the very having been seized I am trying to defend and make manifest. But I am concerned over the fragility of the position of these like-minded "opponents," and am particularly concerned over their morally inaccurate eliding of all nonhuman Faces.

---

3. Most humans can be set apart as the only creatures capable of reading this book and capable of ethical reflection. Infants and very young children, or those who have suffered from debilitating accidents or disease, may not have ethical or even, in extreme cases (e.g., permanent coma), moral capacities. Creatures are only ethically responsible to the degree they are both morally response-able and capable of ethical reflection. We humans find ourselves seized by the Faces of creatures who are not themselves morally response-able and/or ethically responsible (e.g., saplings, cats, infants). Insofar as we are morally response-able and ethically capable, we are ethically responsible even for those who are not ethically or morally culpable (including, obviously, those who cannot reciprocate). In this sense, those who can read and reason over this book bear more moral responsibility than saplings, cats, and infants, and bear responsibility for saplings, cats, and infants.

All Life is Sacred

I am attempting to articulate a theoretically stronger and more accurate account of the moral and the ethical. As has hopefully becoming clear, when I erase the bright moral line distinguishing humans as a class even as I rehabilitate the moral, I reject an untenable position while affirming the sanctity of all life. I am not lessening the power of anyone's sense for the infinite, sacred value of human life. To the contrary, I am defending the sanctity of all life, for I am striving to heighten a sense for the infinite, incomparable, sacred value of each and every living creature.

A World Teeming with Faces

Imagine a world in which everyone had spiritual sensitivities so refined they were attentive to and moved even by the Faces of crickets, worms, and saplings. Imagine the infinite sensitivity so spiritually attuned a population of people would have to the suffering of other people and all other creatures. Imagine how profoundly that moral sensitivity would affect human understanding, decisions, and actions, how it would influence the ways people structure their common life together. When one imagines such a world, a world in which everyone has such refined sensitivities, when one imagines how such a world would be organized, engaged, and loved, one gains a concrete sense for the ethical and political significance of the moral.

Even if everyone's sensitivities were refined by full openness and maximal fidelity to having been seized by love for the Faces of all others, people would still be killing worms and cutting down trees in order to survive. But everyone would be mourning every worm and every sapling. Of course, any suffering, sadness, or falling short of utmost potential for any human would be mourned intensely. All would dream, *per impossibile*, of a day when love and peace and the full flourishing of every creature would cover the earth as the waters cover the seas. All would dream, *per impossibile*, of a day in which spiritual sensitivity to the Face of each and every creature so overwhelmed every creature that none did any harm to any other on all the earth. And all would strive each and every day to see that such a world, if impossible to realize perfectly, was realized on each particular day as fully and richly as possible.

We will never live in such a perfectly good world. But we are nowhere close to maximizing our ability to make the world as good as possible, and it is impossible to think that in such a spiritually attuned world we would not be far more compassionate and careful with every life. That is the potential

Part Three: Beyond Objectivity, Relativism, and Extremism

force of awakening to primordial having been seized by love for the Faces of each and every creature, the potential force of awakening for ethical judgments, convictions, and actions. It is a force for compassion, for sympathy, for sacrifice, and for flourishing and peace on earth. It is a force that would, to paraphrase Emmanuel Levinas, lead people to fear injustice more than death, to prefer to suffer injustice than to commit it, and to prefer what justifies life to what secures it.[4]

Significantly, those filled with this spirit would possess the courage to own their moral convictions fully, and they would not shrink from complete honesty about either their having been seized or the brutal realities of the world. Indeed, as one contemplates our world consumed by this moral sensitivity, the most subtle and spiritually disturbing threat of this position may be felt, for once one opens oneself so fully to all Faces, one feels the threatening possibility that one will be overwhelmed by all the pain and horror suffusing our world. At this juncture, a moral/spiritual abyss becomes visible. The threat, consequences, and challenge of this abyss rise with increasing urgency as the moral sphere is rehabilitated. That is, in the immediate wake of our rehabilitation of the moral, an existential abyss rises up and confronts us: how do we affirm existence and ourselves in this vale of tears? Addressing the challenge of this abyss is beyond the brief of this study.[5] The task here is to rehabilitate moral realism, to reawaken us to agape, that is, to stimulate and defend the reasonableness of awakening to having been seized by love for the Faces of all creatures, and to delineate the ethical implications of this awakening to moral reality.

A Vision of "Ethics" in a Post-Moral World

In the early 1990s I helped to teach a course in biomedical ethics as a "visiting lecturer" at an elite, Ivy League university. The topic for the week was human experimentation. Our main reading was by Hans Jonas.[6] For Jonas, the worst human experimentation is that which involves coercion and lack of concern for experimental subjects. Consider, for instance, a worst-case

---

4. The exact quote is, "The human, or human inwardness, is the return to the inwardness of nonintentional consciousness, to bad conscience, to its possibility of fearing injustice more than death, of preferring injustice undergone to injustice committed, and what justifies being to what secures it" (Levinas, *entre-nous*, 132).

5. I focus upon this challenge in Greenway, *The Challenge of Evil*.

6. Jonas, "Philosophical Reflections on Experimenting with Human Subjects."

example: Nazi scientists experimented upon humans by exposing them to freezing cold water until they died in order to measure human tolerance and response to cold. In this case, there was no concern for the well-being of the subjects, who were utterly and completely coerced (their Faces were utterly discounted).

At an opposite extreme, a best-case example, familiar from the movies, comes when the heroic (emotionally healthy) scientist, out of commitment to her own project, experiments upon herself. Here the subject is fully aware of the risks, fully concerned for herself, but is so fully committed to the experiment and its potential benefits that she is willing to assume the risks and give fully informed, non-coerced consent (e.g., the heroine of the movie is so moved by the Faces of others that she is willing to risk her health in order to test a possible cure).

Jonas concedes that it is typically impractical for scientists to experiment upon themselves. He quite reasonably suggests that nonetheless the extremes provide a reliable ethical guide. In general, human experimentation is more ethical the more voluntary it is, and more evil the less voluntary it is. To truly volunteer involves fully understanding the risks one is taking and taking them for authentic moral reasons (I would argue that an appeal to having been seized by love for Faces is implicit here, though Jonas conducts his argument within standard modern ethical parameters). Thus both a lack of coercion and informed consent (i.e., aspects of love for the Faces of humans that involves respecting their autonomy) is critical.

About fifteen of the forty-five students in my sections of the biomedical ethics class, however, countered in their weekly papers with another "ethic" that I had never before encountered in the guise of an ethic. They called it "social utility theory" (not, let me emphasize, utilitarianism; I do not know where they got the "social utility" moniker, for there is no generally recognized ethic which goes by that name). They argued that it was those who benefited society the least, those with the least "social utility," who should be experimented upon first. That is, not professionals—doctors, lawyers, politicians, teachers or students at elite universities—but those whose contribution was not notable or those who were easily replaced (e.g., those who were more poorly educated, held common or socially marginal jobs, perhaps convicted criminals), those are the folks who should undergo the risks of being experimental subjects. I pushed and asked if they would hold this generally. That is, are people with less social utility to a society also the ones who should be on the front lines in a war, or the last in line when

PART THREE: BEYOND OBJECTIVITY, RELATIVISM, AND EXTREMISM

it comes to expensive or scarce medical treatment? "Yes, of course," came their perfectly consistent reply.

The closest articulated "ethic" that this approaches would be "social Darwinism," which is commonly attributed to Herbert Spencer. In stark contrast to the affirmation that all people are created equal and, for that matter, in stark contrast to the central ethical affirmations of all the world's classic wisdom/faith traditions, social Darwinism affirms as good the "might makes right" dynamics of a survival of the fittest struggle among humans. Social Darwinism has been so universally reviled that Spencer's defenders typically argue that Spencer did not really teach social Darwinism, and most Darwinists also vehemently reject the idea that modern evolutionary theory entails social Darwinism. Nonetheless, in the early 1990s fully a third of my students in a biomedical ethics class at one of the most elite universities in the world openly argued for a form of social Darwinism.

This is but a single example. Significantly, however, my "social utility" students, far more than Jonas, reflect modern social realities. Those who are poorer and less well educated are most likely to end up in the front lines of our wars, very often out of financial need (a form of coercion), not because of ethical ideals (note how often United States military advertising itself focuses not upon the military's role in protecting and furthering American ethical ideals, but upon vocational and personal benefits).[7] Pharmaceutical companies typically experiment upon "volunteers" who are poorly educated and in need of money (as advertisements recruiting subjects for medical experiments make abundantly clear).[8] Such examples can easily be multiplied (to cite just a few examples, think in terms of quality of legal representation, access to quality health care, or the diverse quality of basic educational opportunities). And by this point it is clear how brutally modern society tends to maximize the utility of those who are utterly marginal and without voice, namely, nonhuman animals.

---

7. Let me stress that I am aware that many soldiers, including some of my students, enlist because of their ideals or out of fidelity to family tradition. My position does not discount such individuals, it worries that their admirable idealism is being exploited.

8. Let me stress that I am not comparing modern medical experimentation on humans with the Nazis. There is a broad continuum here, and much modern research requires oversight from independent ethics boards and is highly ethical and important, even life-saving. Nonetheless, it is important in each of these cases to name the *de facto* realities and to keep track of the ways in which they are in practice reflecting the realization of a public "ethic" in which people are treated as commodities in accord with their socioeconomic status.

All Life is Sacred

Let me be sure to stress that many students in my class were going into medicine, law, or other fields because of their desire to help people and create a good society. A number of them had decided to go into medicine because they had been seized by love for Faces. For them, medicine truly was still a sort of ministry to those in need—though the degree to which such idealistic students are able to stay true to their ideals within the modern medical industry is a significant question. On the other hand, the "social utility" third of my students and their like-minded peers are also out there in society. Given their undeniable intelligence (most of the "social utility" students were very bright) and their Ivy League pedigree, these "social utility" enthusiasts are most likely wielding considerable political and cultural power within our society, and acting in accord with the tenets of social Darwinism.

Part Four

PERFECT LOVE IN AN IMPERFECT WORLD
Agape Ethics

CHAPTER 10

Moral Sensitivity, Ethical Judgment, Ethical Conviction

I have been striving to make clear how the rehabilitation of the moral leads across the board, and hopefully with increasing influence in the world, to incredible sensitivity to the sanctity of all life. I also explained, however, why primordial, moral, having been seized provides no basis for discriminating ethically between a human boy, a worm, a sapling, and a cat. This made clear the radical implications of the incommensurability between the sphere of the moral and the sphere of the ethical, especially in light of the recognition that people are not only seized by the Faces of humans.

In these closing chapters I strive to defend the idea that while, on the one hand, there is no *moral* distinction between the cat and the boy there is, on the other hand, a massive *ethical* distinction between the cat and the boy. I strive to delineate the character and force of ethical judgments for ethical convictions, and also begin very roughly to map what will ultimately be, at many points, the irreducibly fuzzy relationship between the moral and the ethical.

Let me pause to stress that while of necessity I will broach significant ethical issues, and while in some instances my mapping of the moral/ethical relationship already suggests distinct positions on controversial issues, I will remain true to the focus upon the moral/ethical relation and not succumb to the temptation to engage in detailed ethical analysis and argument vis-à-vis any particular controversy. Such ethical analysis and argument is of critical importance, but it remains beyond the parameters of this study.

Part Four: Perfect Love in an Imperfect World

This chapter is inescapably technical and abstract insofar as its task is to map the contours of the relation among moral sensitivity, ethical judgment, and ethical conviction. Fortunately, the contours of this map will become clearer in the following chapter as I flesh out the outlines of our mapping of the moral and ethical in relation to concrete ethical challenges.

The inescapable role of ethical judgment

Suppose I am faced with the ability to intervene in a situation where either a boy or a cat will be killed. I contend that if someone would decide in that instance to save the cat or leave things to chance, they evidence profound ethical confusion. A small cadre of opponents would immediately attack this position, accusing me of bias towards humans. They would suggest that there is no valid moral basis for privileging the life of the boy over the life of the cat. They would argue that I privilege the life of the boy because I am a fellow human and am thus biased toward humans and criteria that reflect human prejudices by privileging human capacities (e.g., the ability to reflect, to be creative, to exercise free will, or to form complex family and social relationships).

I would respond that I am not simply biased, for my ethical conviction is wholly reasonable. Moreover, and this is the critical point, *all morality, insofar as it enters the world, is immediately ethical, and so the identification of any Face as a particular face (e.g., human, cat, sapling), an identification that carries an inextricably comparative content, in fact and immediately brings ethical judgment into play*. One voids the ethical when one denies the moral, for the moral lies at the heart of all true ethics. Nonetheless, one cannot deny the significance and force of ethical judgment. And this means noticing and affirming the inextricably reasoned character of all ethical judgment. Precisely speaking, one by definition never makes a *moral* judgment. There is only *ethical* judgment. For all *judgments* that follow upon the *moral reality* of having been seized by love for Faces are *ethical*, for all judgments happen in history and involve reasoning, while the moral is outside of history and reasoning. So every ethical conviction is rooted in *having been seized by love* (the moral), but since every ethical conviction is historical and reasoned, every *ethical conviction* also inextricably involves *ethical judgment*.

In particular, then, I would meet my opponents' objections by specifying ethically pertinent distinctions. I would argue that the boy, in stark contrast to the cat, has vastly superior capacities to reason, to create, to form relationships, to love, to appreciate beauty, family, friends, art, literature, and so forth, though I would note that such abilities are not wholly lacking in the cat. This distinction in capacities, I would argue, makes the awful violation of the death of the boy ethically far worse than the awful violation of the death of the cat. That is, the death of the cat and the death of the boy would both be infinitely awful *morally*, but the death of the boy would be *ethically* far worse than the death of the cat. Thus, I would conclude, one most definitely *should* act to save the boy, though one should also most definitely mourn the cat, and I acknowledge that one is caught here having to choose among bad options (i.e., choose such that the boy is killed, the cat is killed, or choose to leave matters to chance).

My opponents, however, could immediately object that with such appeals I am only confirming their suspicion that I am illicitly invoking anthropocentric criteria. Indeed, they might point out, it is illicit and inconsistent, given the primordial character of the moral, for me to invoke any criteria at all. Life as such, they would insist, is sacred. The Face of the cat is just as sacred, just as immeasurable, as the life of the boy, and thus I should refuse to intervene when faced with such an alternative. Overwhelmed by the moral incomparability of Faces, I should leave matters to chance.

For the reasons just given, I think my opponents' objection is ethically mistaken. But because of the ineffable, infinite character of our having been seized, their objection should not be ridiculed. To the contrary, not only insofar as the immeasurable, sacred character of the having been seized by love for the Faces of others is concerned, but also with regard to the morally problematic character of my appeal to the superior capacities of the boy in comparison to the cat, *my opponents make a critical and correct moral point*. It is important for me explicitly to concede and never to forget this, for precisely this admission protects against any temptation to protect a sense of innocence or even affirm unmitigated privilege by eliding the moral altogether.

One should remember that there is no hierarchy in play in the transcending having been seized by love for the Face of any face. Taken in isolation—just me and my cat, just me and the writhing squirrel I just hit despite slamming on the brakes—each and every Face seizes you immediately, absolutely, infinitely. In terms of having been seized (the moral), there is no distinction between the boy, the cat, the worm, and the sapling.

Nonetheless, every Face appears with a face (i.e., in history), and insofar as we exist in history we never encounter or identify the face of a Face in isolation. The face (human, cat, sapling) of every Face is encountered in history, within the boundaries of thought, in inextricably comparative contexts. In history, in the world, when making ethical judgments, reasoned, comparative, and contextual factors are in fact in play and informing ethical conviction. Both having been seized (moral reality) and ethical judgments, then, are essential aspects of ethical conviction. Ethical convictions, existing as they do *in* history, are illegitimate/empty when they possess no moral dimension. At the same time, ethical convictions, existing as they do *in* history, are illegitimate/in denial when they forget the reality and significance of ethical judgments (i.e., of their historical, reasoned dimension).[1]

Returning to our example, I impose a hierarchy—a contingent, reasoned hierarchy—when I privilege the boy. This is both a compromise upon the purity of the moral and ethically inescapable. For people do not exist in the moral realm alone, people exist *in* history, in the reasoned sphere of ethical judgment, and so people's ethical convictions are always the product not merely of having been seized but also of ethical judgment. Those who would not privilege the boy over the cat forget the inescapability of ethical judgment, they forget that insofar as they too are in history they cannot but be making an ethical (reasoned, comparative) judgment in the case of the boy and the cat, and so both their implicit denial that they are involved in making ethical judgments, and their correlate refusal to attend to distinctions even in this case, where the distinctions are relatively extreme, is indefensible and unethical.

The distinctions between a cat and a boy are fairly extreme. Thus people can enjoy great surety regarding their ethical judgments in this case (which, as should be abundantly clear by now, most certainly does not stop you from mourning the cat). This example, however, explores only one site on a continuous plane of moral/ethical interaction that I will roughly map in order to round out my account of the relations among having been seized (moral reality), ethical judgment, and ethical conviction. I will now generate several examples that will begin to make the contour of the plane of moral/ethical interaction more visible.

---

1. In theological terms, we might speak of all this in terms of a "fall" into knowledge and history, and of a calling to be in the world but not of it.

Moral Sensitivity, Ethical Judgment, Ethical Conviction

Illustrations

Say, to use a very serious and disturbing example, that instead of a choice between a boy and cat, one is faced with a choice between two boys, and that one is presented with the same sort of criteria that I invoked to defend prioritizing the boy over the cat. For instance, one boy has superior capacities to reason, create, form relationships, love, appreciate beauty, family, friends, art, literature, and so forth. The other boy has suffered a horrible brain injury and is severely challenged physically and mentally. Each of the boys is in equally desperate need of a heart transplant in order to survive the week. There is one heart available, and it is equally suitable for either boy. Assuming all relevant factors aside from those specified are equal (e.g., each got onto the transplant list on the same day, chances of success are equal, and so forth), which boy gets the heart transplant, the multi-talented or the challenged, or does one let chance decide?

I would strongly argue that in this case we should refuse to allow any criteria involving capacities to intervene, that when faced with a choice among such similar faces of Faces we should flip a coin and let chance decide. The degree of distinction between the faces, I would argue, does not rise to notice before the blazing moral incomparability of each of their Faces. Just as dim stars vanish in the shining brilliance of a full moon, at this low level of distinction we remain so overwhelmed by the bright light of our having been seized by each boy's Face that minor ethical considerations do not come into view. Where the brilliance of the moral outshines such relatively minor distinctions, there is inadequate basis for reasoned discrimination, so the correct action is to refrain from discriminating, to let chance decide.

However, with regard to this particular case some people who would otherwise generally be considered to be good and reasonable may disagree. They would argue, on the basis of the same criteria that I invoked above with regard to the cat, that while the death of either boy would be morally awful, the death of the multi-talented boy would be ethically worse, and thus that one should give the heart to the multi-talented boy. I would respond, now taking a stance akin to my opponents in the boy/cat scenario above, that every human life is sacred, is of infinite value. So, again, when faced with this situation, I contend that we should remain so overwhelmed by the incomparability of the Faces that we refuse to intervene with any logic, for in contrast to the case contrasting the cat and the boy, the ethical distinctions here are far too slight to rise to notice before the blazing brightness of the incomparable Faces.

Now, despite my strong personal feelings, I believe this represents a case over which in reality there would be widespread disagreement (this in contrast to the cat versus boy example, where I do not anticipate widespread disagreement). I fear, however, that disagreement with the position that I advocate in this case would be related primarily to the eliding of the moral and the commodifying of life in modern thought. At any rate, now let us modify the example to create two more positions with regard to which I do not think there would be significant, if any, disagreement.

In this second case the choice is between a healthy boy and a boy in a coma from which there is no reasonable expectation of recovery. In this case, in addition to the coma the second boy has an untreatable cancer that will surely kill him within one or two weeks. Now what do we do when asked who gets the heart, the healthy boy or the late-term, terminally ill boy in the irremediable coma?

At this point, with deep angst, based upon a contrast in capacities, I argue we should intervene and give the heart to the healthy boy and not to the late-term, terminally ill boy in the irremediable coma. I find even imagining myself doing this deeply disturbing—clearly this is a choice among bad options—but nonetheless I would find that at this extreme the distinctions possess an ethical significance that comes clearly into view despite my enduring moral sensibilities.

I can shift the example to an opposite extreme. Instead of one boy terminally ill and comatose, in this example the only difference between the boys is a moderate variation in academic performance in school. Now what do we do when asked who gets the heart? Here classic ethical convictions are as sure as they are in the case of the boy and the cat, the slight distinction in academic performance does not even begin to come into view in the light of our blazing having been seized by the incomparability of the Faces. Chance should decide.

Along another tack, we can shift nothing about the faces of the Faces, but vary the stakes. As with the last example, in this example the only difference between the boys is a moderate variation in academic performance in school. But instead of the stakes being life and death, at question is the awarding of a prize for academic achievement. Even here an ethical question remains in play: can and should we publicly value some students more than others based on academic achievement? Assuming students are also being valued in other ways, the limited ethical stakes here would suggest that vis-à-vis the bestowing of an academic award it is appropriate to use even a moderate distinction in academic performance as a basis for distinguishing between two faces of Faces.

For the next case, alter the boy/cat example. In this case, one finds the boy enjoying himself and establishing "street cred" with his four-year-old friends by using a magnifying glass and the sun's rays to burn a worm. Here, since the stakes for the worm are life and death and the stakes for the boy are, at best, inconsequential, I contend we should intervene to help the worm. In a complex way that could inform the character of our intervention, it is possible that one should also intervene in order to help salvage and nurture the moral awakening and ethical judgment of the boy.

Are there life-and-death scenarios in which one would privilege nonhuman over human life? Though there are plenty of scenarios in which humans should exercise restraint or even sacrifice mightily for the sake of nonhuman animals, I admit that I cannot think of a realistic life-and-death scenario in which I would expect widespread agreement (or would argue personally) for privileging nonhuman over human life. It is not difficult, however, to construct fanciful scenarios with regard to which I would expect widespread agreement. Say, for instance, that one is in a situation where one can act either to save the life of a man or act to prevent a toxic spill that will surely kill the five hundred remaining members of an endangered species of whales. The man is ninety-three, comatose, gravely ill, and expected to die within hours or, at most, days. He was celebrated for dedicating his life to preservation of critical habitat for endangered species and was for many years the leader of the World Wildlife Fund. In this case, I would expect broad agreement that we should act to prevent the toxic spill even if it means not saving the man.

Principles of moral/ethical relations

Now let me use the analysis of these various cases in order roughly to delineate principles of the relationship between the moral and the ethical. First and foremost, each of our responses involves having been seized by love for the Face of each and every face (i.e., agape, the moral). Even in the first example, where I absolutely privilege the life of the boy over the life of the cat, the sense that I am making a painful ethical judgment (no matter how sure) and my mourning of the cat signals the enduring reality of the moral. Failure truly to mourn the cat would indicate that the "ethical" decision lacked a moral dimension and so was not truly ethical—the essential and ever-present character of the moral dimension means that one should always consider the spiritual character of any ethical decision and action to be critical.

Second, as the case of boy/cat also illustrates, when there is a radical distinction among faces and the stakes for the privileged face are high (e.g., life and death), the significance of the distinctions will be so great that they will shine through with decisive ethical consequences. While I am seized both by the Face of the boy and the Face of the cat, the distinctions between their faces are so profound that they shine through with significant influence, and so I make an ethical judgment and privilege the life of the boy.

Third, as the case of boy/worm/magnifying glass illustrates, when there is a radical distinction among faces but the stakes for each face vary, the ethical priority of the privileged face is far from absolute. Here again one is seized by both Faces, and one notes the radical distinction between the faces, but one also takes account of the differing stakes for each face. When the boy's autonomy and desire for "street cred" are weighed against the suffering and potential death of the worm, the well-being of the worm takes priority (as noted, one might also be motivated by concern for the boy's moral awakening).

Fourth, as variations on the scenarios with the two boys illustrates, the same factors that are vital vis-à-vis the boy and the cat are also vital vis-à-vis the two boys. As the distinctions between the faces of the boys became more or less pronounced, and in relation to the stakes involved, comparative considerations played more or less of a role. When the stakes were high (i.e., human life and death) and the distinction between faces was slight (i.e., moderate academic distinction), I concluded that ethical distinctions did not shine though the brilliance of primordial, moral, having been seized. However, when the stakes were low (i.e., bestowal of an academic award) and the distinction between faces was slight (i.e., moderate academic achievement), even slight distinctions shone through as significant.

I contended strongly that the distinctions still did not shine through even when the distinction between faces was greater (multi-talented versus challenged boy), but, admittedly, as the distinctions become even greater there will be more ambiguity regarding when distinctions between faces are great enough for ethical considerations to come into play. At points in the

Moral Sensitivity, Ethical Judgment, Ethical Conviction

scenarios the distinction between the faces became so great (i.e., boy who is healthy versus boy with late-stage, terminal illness and in coma) that the significance of the distinctions shone through strongly.

Quandary ethics cases reside in the gray lands between the relative extremes, where the level of distinction among the faces of Faces and variations in the stakes combine to make ethical judgment ambiguous and contentious (e.g., at some point in a life-and-death scenario, along the continuum between the second boy being slightly less academically able to the second boy being in an irremediable coma and about to die of a terminal disease, everyone will stumble across what is for them an ethically gray area). Agape ethics can locate cases upon a continuum from "great" to "no" ethical surety, and can provide a sense for why gray area cases present irremediable ethical quandaries, but agape ethics no more than any other can provide magical shortcuts that enable people to determine what is right in quandary cases. Nonetheless, again, by placing these cases on a moral/ethical plane, agape ethics clarifies why such cases present irremediable ethical quandaries even for people with great moral sensitivity and exquisite ethical judgment. Perhaps that understanding can help all of us to be gracious both toward others and toward ourselves when we find ourselves forced to respond in grave and ambiguous contexts (e.g., end of life decisions for a loved one) where we must make crushing decisions without the comfort of ethical surety.

It should go without saying that I am making no attempt to be exhaustive here even with regard to the relations among the moral and the ethical, let alone vis-à-vis the multitude of contemporary areas of complicated ethical reflection. But given the significance of this rehabilitation of the moral when taken in combination with an analysis that erases the bright moral line between humans and all other species, and given my affirmation of the difference in kind between the moral and the ethical, it was incumbent upon me to clarify how the moral affects the ethical and at least very roughly to begin to map the irreducibly but not totally fuzzy relationship between the moral and the ethical.

IN SUM: AGAPE (MORAL REALITY), ETHICAL JUDGMENT, ETHICAL CONVICTION

The major features of a neo-Levinasian agape ethic are now in general view. First and foremost, there is rehabilitation of the moral itself, which lies at the root of and motivates all genuine ethics. Second, there is the inclusion of all life, not just human life, within the scope of moral concern, that is, there is an affirmation that we are seized not only by the Faces of other humans, but also by the Faces of crickets, seals, whales, cats, and saplings. As a consequence of these first two factors, third, there is a powerful shift toward treasuring every life as invaluable, as sacred.

Fourth, there is recognition that people live in history, and so there is an affirmation that ethical judgments based upon distinctions among the faces of Faces are an inextricable part of every ethical conviction, and play a legitimate and determinative role when circumstance forces us ethically to compare moral incomparables.

Fifth, variations between two key ethical factors (i.e., distinctions among faces of Faces, variations in the stakes) can appear in forms and combinations that do not allow for ethical surety. In the midst of such quandary cases, serious ethical reflection and analysis is absolutely critical as we attempt to be as wise and discerning as is possible (and here we would turn to the excellent and tightly focused arguments in ethics developed over the course of the twenty and twenty-first centuries). Vis-à-vis such quandary cases, moreover, generosity and tolerance towards oneself and others should be the rule, for in these cases not even the most morally sensitive and wise among us has access to ethical surety. Notably, this means that inevitably in some high-stakes situations people will be forced in real time to make momentous decisions where there is no possibility of ethical surety.

Finally, all ethical conviction (no matter how sure or unsure) is a product of both having been seized (the moral) and ethical judgment. This realization has been sealed as I have reacted to two decidedly unethical stances. On the one hand, there is the stance of those who deny the reality of ethical judgment (e.g., the stance of those who will not privilege the boy over the cat). On the other hand, there is the stance of those who elide the moral altogether (e.g., the devastating modern confusion I critique throughout this work). Notably, the first of these unethical stances at least has the virtue of being moral.

In the final chapter I will further clarify the character of agape ethics and the relation of the moral and the ethical in conversation with the question of the ethics of killing nonhuman animals. Here again, while my rehabilitation of the moral and delineation of the relation among having been seized by love for the Faces of all others (i.e., agape, moral reality), ethical judgment, and ethical conviction does not eliminate quandary cases, it does with considerable specificity mark out a range of ethical convictions that are clear-cut and sure, and that frame the quandary cases.

Chapter 11

Comparing Incomparables
Killing Nonhuman Creatures

Mapping the Moral and Ethical in Relation to Killing Nonhuman Creatures

In this concluding chapter I attempt to illustrate the ethical consequences of our all-inclusive rehabilitation of the moral in conversation with the issue of the killing of nonhuman creatures. To reiterate, my goal is not to delve into detailed ethical analysis, and I no more than anyone else can provide magical shortcuts to vexing quandary cases. However, the general ways and, with regard to non-quandary cases, the quite specific and definitive ways in which the argument's rehabilitation of the moral influences ethical reflection on these issues should become clear.

I turn in this chapter to the issue of killing nonhuman creatures. Before I begin, let me specify the obvious. In the next few pages I will not even begin to approach an analysis of all the various complicated scenarios or investigate all the subtle nuances that would be essential to any full-scale ethical reflection on the killing of nonhuman creatures. Moreover, even with regard to what I do say, a sense of inadequacy and unseemly brevity will haunt my analysis. There is not space to do more and, given the obvious significance of rehabilitation of the moral for this major ethical

Comparing Incomparables

issue, neither can I avoid at least gesturing toward the ways in which rehabilitation of moral reality influences understanding of the ethics of killing nonhuman creatures.

First, consider several scenarios in which the question is whether or not a person should kill a deer. In scenario[Live] a human kills the deer in order to live. In scenario[Pleasure] a human kills the deer for pleasure. In scenario[Experiment] a human kills the deer in the course of a medical experiment critical for saving human lives or for preventing dire human suffering. In scenario[Cosmetic] a human kills the deer for the sake of a nonmedical cosmetic product. In scenario[Species] a human kills a deer as part of an effort to protect an endangered species threatened by an overpopulation of deer.

I begin with the moral, with having been seized by love for the Face of the human, of course, but also with having been seized by love for the Face of the deer. I should in every instance desire and strive to help the deer to flourish and to enjoy life. It is never good to kill the deer. We should only harm or kill the deer if forced by tragic circumstances involving other Faces, circumstances that force us to compare incomparables, circumstances that force ethical judgments concerning the faces of Faces into play (that is, circumstances that force us to draw ethical comparisons among moral incomparables). The killing will be an act of violence that violates absolutely a morally invaluable Face. The deer will lose its life, and we, its killers, will be morally harmed, our innocence rent, insofar as we must now live in the wake and memory of having violated that Face absolutely. We must now live aware of the fact that we are killers.

Ethically, the deer is a relatively sophisticated creature capable of making basic decisions, enjoying life, having a family, living in community, and feeling pain and fear. One would need biologists to make precise comparisons, but using even lay understanding we can affirm with surety along a hierarchy of ethical value that the violation of the Face of the deer is ethically worse than the violation of the Face of a dandelion and ethically better than the violation of the Face of a human.

In scenario[Live], accordingly, we should violate the Face of the deer by hunting and killing him or her if and only if that were necessary to provide essential nourishment for ourselves or our families, for the distinctions between the faces of the deer and our own or our families' human faces are significant enough to shine through having been seized by the Faces of the deer and of ourselves or our families, and to create a clear ethical privilege for us humans. Indeed, given the large distinction between the faces of deer

PART FOUR: PERFECT LOVE IN AN IMPERFECT WORLD

and of humans, we should judge it unethical ever to privilege the life of the deer over the life of a human where the stakes for both deer and human are life and death.

Even in this case, where the killing of the deer is judged ethical, the *spirit* of the hunt is critical, determining our spiritual state, and guiding us ethically. While remaining moral and ethical, we may enjoy the woods, the utilization of navigation and tracking skills, or perhaps the camaraderie with friends and family, but we do not enjoy or relish the kill. There is no blood lust, no flush of satisfaction, no empowerment, no bragging over the kill. Because of our love for the deer, we kill as painlessly and efficiently as possible. We do not kill the strongest deer, a mother deer with her children, or choose the deer with the biggest antlers. We choose deer that are older or injured and unlikely to survive long in any case.

The ethical necessity of killing the deer is never an excuse for doing something that we want to do anyway, for there is no desire to kill, no pleasure in the kill. To the contrary, we only kill, only suffer the act of violating that Face, if and only if we are driven to it out of fidelity to other Faces in a context where we are forced to compare incomparables and make ourselves into killers.

The act of the kill is so awe-full/awful, so significant, that some liturgy should be felt to be necessary by any genuinely moral person in order to acknowledge the evil and to help one cope with the reality of the violation. We might take a moment over the deer's body to acknowledge explicitly the tragic character of life in this world, where at times we must kill in order to live, where at times the ethical violates the moral. We might speak aloud of the deer's life and of its value, we might name the Faces that drive us to this action, and name the good that the deer's killing will accomplish for those Faces. We might place our hands on the deer, inhabit the awfulness of the violation, and (whether or not we believe in God) utter a cry of pain, of sorrow, a cry for forgiveness, for grace. For despite the fact that we judge the killing to be the best ethical option in forced circumstances, it is nonetheless an absolute moral violation.

Let us stress that we have not *sacrificed* the life of the deer. While we do indeed sacrifice in this scenario, what we sacrifice, for the sake of human Faces, is fidelity to the Face of the deer. We sacrifice our moral purity. The death of the deer is not that sacrifice. One can only sacrifice oneself. When someone decides someone else's fate, kills someone else, the other one, the victim, has not made a sacrifice, for their hand has been forced. The deer did not sacrifice its life. The deer wanted to live and probably sought as best as possible to avoid our bullets. So we should not subtly and illicitly deny the harsh moral reality by speaking of the necessity of *sacrificing* the life of the deer.

While with these qualifications we should affirm the killing of the deer in scenario^{Live}, where killing the deer is necessary for human survival, there is never justification for killing the deer in scenario^{Pleasure}, where we kill the deer for pleasure. We may gain a demonic rush of power and sense of superiority from the kill, but this is a *demonic* rush, for it runs against agape. This demonic rush of power feeds a perversity of spirit. For we who are moral, there is never pleasure in the kill.

On the other hand, scenario^{Experiment}, when we kill the deer in the course of a critical medical experiment, is akin to scenario^{Live}, where we kill so that a human may live. Insofar as the experiment is necessary in order to save human lives or to prevent dire human suffering or is ethically the best alternative for gaining essential medical information (life-saving, no alternatives), we should consider it ethical to experiment upon the deer.

All the qualifications that pertained to scenario^{Live}, however, would also apply to scenario^{Experiment}, with the experimenter now standing in the place of the hunter. Notably, this commends the use of liturgies helping all honestly to name and to cope with the tragic realities. Face-eliding talk of "animal resources" would be condemned (I teach across the street from the "animal resources" building of a major university; and of course we would also want to reflect upon the equally troubling ramifications of the rhetoric of "human resources"). Here again, we should reject common and illicit talk of the "sacrifice" experimental subjects are making. Scientists should also drop reality-twisting talk of the "privilege" of working with nonhuman others who have no voice in their fate. One should remain fully alive to the grim fact that nonhuman creatures who are the subjects of medical experimentation are unwilling subjects forced to suffer and/or die so that others might gain. Finally and obviously, wherever possible one should minimize the pain and suffering and maximize the life potentials of every experimental subject.[1]

Of course, much medical experimentation is not related to essential medical knowledge, and at the far end of this continuum one shades into

---

1. For a far more detailed exploration of animal experimentation, an exploration that makes it unclear whether or not the ethical criteria I am claiming would be required to justify animal experimentation can ever be met, see Linzey and Linzey, eds., *Normalising the Unthinkable*.

experimentation that is not related to serious medical conditions at all but to scenario^{Cosmetic}, where one afflicts or kills the deer for the sake of cosmetic or nonessential procedures and products. Scenario^{Cosmetic} is really just a species of scenario^{Pleasure}, where one is killing the deer for the sake of pleasure. For obvious reasons, rehabilitation of the moral precludes any experimentation upon animals for purely cosmetic reasons.

To be sure, the line between "medically essential" and "cosmetic" is not absolutely clear, nor will all agree about the boundaries of "dire human suffering," nor upon what degree of torture of subjects is justified by what degree of potential aid to human Faces, nor over how to compare the faces of the Faces of deer versus cows, pigs, rabbits, mice, or monkeys. In ways that should be clear by this point, such factors can combine to create considerable ethical ambiguity, and at such junctures careful ethical reflection on a case-by-case basis is essential. My approach does not offer anything definitive to the resolution of such ambiguous cases, but it does clarify the issues at stake by recognizing such areas of intractable ambiguity—and again, no one has any magical shortcut that resolves quandary cases. Significantly, my approach does require that all participants in the ethical discussion genuinely love every creature and be wholly concerned to do nothing that is not necessitated in a context where one is forced ethically to compare moral incomparables.

Scenario^{Species} is an especially ambiguous type of case because it requires adjudicating between an individual (or, more likely, numerous individuals) and a species. Since ecological diversity is of value to the flourishing and survival of multitudes of individuals, the threat of extinction is highly significant and carries considerable moral weight in comparison to the flourishing or death of an individual or group of individuals from a non-endangered species (e.g., when an "invasive" species—roughly, a species which is introduced into an otherwise discrete ecosystem by artificial means—is wiping out an indigenous species). But all pertinent factors should here again be weighed carefully on a case-by-case basis.

Agape Ethics

Although this defense and unfolding of agape ethics is obviously not even close to being comprehensive, by this point the ethical significance of the rehabilitation of the moral for the judgments and actions of humans, as well as the essence, legitimacy, and public significance of agape ethics should be

Comparing Incomparables

emerging clearly. First, the reality of the moral can be affirmed *publicly*; the reality of agape is not merely a matter of personal preference or opinion. Second, it follows that those who are amoral or immoral can be publicly judged to be insensitive to a profound reality. Third, only those who are awakened to having been seized by love for the Faces of all creatures are morally qualified to engage in ethical debate. Fourth, all who are moral will own wholly and articulate clearly their passionate desire to remain fully faithful to every Face. Fifth, everyone who is moral will sense the tragedy and moral awfulness of injuring any Face. Sixth, none who are moral will decide to act violently against any Face unless they are absolutely compelled to do so because they are forced, *per impossibile*, to compare incomparables.

Not only will our rehabilitation of the moral profoundly affect the spirit of ethical debate, then, but also certain practices that today are commonly accepted or are the source of supposedly ethical debate should clearly fall beyond the pale. For instance, everyone should immediately reject trophy hunting, canned hunts (where a nonhuman animal is released in confined quarters so someone can shoot him or her), hunting for pleasure, eating dishes that involve needless animal suffering (e.g., veal, *foie gras*, factory farmed chickens and pigs), eating any animal (especially members of advanced species) beyond what is required by profound need, or testing or exploiting animals for cosmetic reasons (from lipstick to food coloring to fur coats), and everyone should be concerned to preserve habitats and ecosystems, even if it is solely nonhuman creatures who are being saved and enhanced.

While my position does not resolve quandary cases, then, it does significantly clarify the boundaries of the quandary cases and should affect one's sense for the moral spirit of all ethical reflection. The sacred character of every Face remains wholly and continually before us. Moreover, insofar as I have delineated ethical positions that anyone who is moral will clearly affirm (in contrast to issues about which no one can have ethical surety, which is not to be confused with personal passion), I have justified criteria for public ethics that do not turn upon the impossible, modern demand for objective, universal, and indubitable knowledge and, accordingly, I have delineated ethical judgments that should be inscribed into the public policies of any good society.

Part Four: Perfect Love in an Imperfect World

Spiritual Discipline and Spiritual Awakening: Two Final People Tales

Insofar as people reflexively kill crickets, insofar as they fail to find joy in the tale of Kiki, insofar as they remain closed off from love for *all* creatures, they are lost, alienated from moral reality. For having been seized by love for the Faces of all creatures, that is, awakening to agape, lies at the heart of moral reality. Agape opens us to the most profound and meaningful dimensions of reality. Yes, agape opens us to profound sorrow and sadness—that is reality—but agape also opens us to profound joy and to the essence of the meaningfulness of life. Predominant streams of modern Western rationality alienate people from agape, from moral reality, from other creatures, from profound joy, fellowship, sorrow, and sadness, from the very meaningfulness of life. As a consequence of influential streams of modern Western rationality the world is disenchanted, hollowed out, and we are left with a cold vision of atomistic egos pursuing individual desires for pleasure, security, and power in a war of all against all.

My prime focus in this work has been upon spiritual awakening to agape. For the sake of humans and all creatures, I hope that people might be awakened by what is, happily, an increasingly vibrant and widespread struggle to reawaken in humans a lost source of spiritual comfort and joy. My desire is to reawaken a lost sense of spiritual belonging in this world, to retrieve a lost sense of communion with all creatures and all creation, and to return us to a morally realistic, ethically responsible, and truly spiritual living of life.

More than a decade ago Adriana studied creation spirituality with me. A few years later she came back to campus and complained happily that her two daughters had pretty much become vegetarian. She explained that as a way of paying attention her husband, her daughters, and she had begun to name all the faces on the table when they said grace before meals. When they knew their food had come from workers laboring in oppressive conditions in fields or processing plants, they began to name those unknown workers as well. As they began with this spiritual discipline to *attend*, they began to find themselves really saying grace, pleading for grace, for they often found themselves eating the well-being of others, sometimes the very flesh of others, in a broken world.

Over time, as Adriana's family paused daily to say grace, as they paused before each meal and explicitly acknowledged the Faces of all the faces that, directly or indirectly, lay on their table, they began to be transformed by agape. They soon found themselves passionately desiring to eat at a table that involved as little harm and as much love for all creatures as was possible.

Adriana and her family exemplify the spiritual transformation that comes from having been seized by love for the Faces of all creatures. Such spiritual transformation leads one quite happily to act towards every creature as lovingly as possible. Such transformation enriches life with the meaningfulness of love. Truly, as Albert Schweitzer observed, if one loves all Faces, existence will "become harder . . . in every respect than it would be if one lived for oneself." At the same time, as Schweitzer immediately went on to say, "it will be richer, more beautiful, and happier. It will become, instead of mere living, a real experience of life."[2]

Agape is not something we first give or create. It is a gift the awakened first receive. It fills hearts with joy and life with meaningfulness, and it spurs loving action. In having been seized by love for the Faces of all faces, we find that we have been given the gift of love, the gift of meaningful life—sometimes joyous, sometimes painful, but always profoundly meaningful life—and quite reasonably and quite consistently we are moved to strive to live as lovingly as possible in our broken world.

My wife, Cindy, was not initially as enthusiastic as I about nonhuman animal concerns. Many years ago she rushed into my study shouting "Ants, there are ants all over the kitchen!" I hopped up and we walked quickly to the kitchen and sure enough, there were lots of ants. They were coming in through a tiny hole beside the window, crawling down over the overhanging lip of the windowsill, down the wall to the floor, and then five feet across to one of the cat's bowls of food. "Where's the Raid?" Cindy asked. "I'm not sure we have any," I replied, "but let's take a look at them." So we moved in closer to take a look at the ants.

It turned out that there were two distinct lines, pretty exact paths, actually, which every ant followed in and out. And they worked in teams of five, always five, sometimes with a roaming substitute, to get each morsel of cat food out over the lip of the bowl, across the floor, up and over that overhanging windowsill and then out by the window. They tended to spin around each piece of cat food as they carried it, and there was always quite a pause as they struggled over the overhang, but they always made it. They were amazing. And suddenly the Raid didn't seem like so easy a solution.

2. Schweitzer, *Out of My Life and Thought*, 268.

Part Four: Perfect Love in an Imperfect World

Well, they weren't crossing any table or counter space, they weren't into any of our food, we were in a middle of a drought, so they were probably desperate for food, and the cats didn't seem to mind, so I suggested that we wait and see if the ants might get their fill and go away.

Now, the next morning I was leaving for three weeks, so Cindy might have suspected she was getting the raw end of the deal, but she was game, and she agreed to wait and see. As I called to check in over the next week she had more and more detailed stories about the feats of the ants. By the end of the week she told me they had left, and they've not been back since. That was a beginning.

A couple of years later, Cindy said something that told me that quietly and attentively she had been working indirectly but decisively ever since the encounter with the ants, she added her own confession to the confession of having been seized by love for all Faces that lies at the heart of Jewish, Christian, and so many other faiths and spiritualities, to the confession of love to which St. Francis, Albert Schweitzer, Theodor Adorno, Isaac Bashevis Singer, Alice Walker, Sallie McFague, Andrew Linzey, and, for that matter, Isaiah, Jesus, the Buddha, and Ghandi, among innumerable others across spiritual traditions and throughout history, all testify. Cindy testified to the joy and reality of having been seized by love for the Faces of all faces. She walked into our house and said, "a squirrel ran in front of my car this morning." And I said, "Oh, I'm sorry, did you run over the squirrel?" She said, "No, I didn't run over the squirrel, it just ran across the road ahead of me." She paused for a moment. She did not use agape ethics' talk about the moral reality of having been seized by love for a Face, but she said the same thing when she added, "I loved the squirrel. There was nothing special about it, but I loved it."

Bibliography

Adorno, Theodor. *Minima Moralia*. New York: Verso, 2005.
Brooke, John H. *Science and Religion: Some Historical Perspectives*. New York: Cambridge University Press, 1991.
Burtt, Edwin A. *Metaphysical Foundations of Modern Science*. New York: Doubleday, 1954.
Butterfield, Herbert. *The Origins of Modern Science*. Rev. ed. New York: The Free Press, 1997.
Dawkins, Richard. *The Extended Phenotype: The Long Reach of the Gene*. Oxford: Oxford University Press, 1999.
———. *The Selfish Gene*. Oxford: Oxford University Press, 1999.
De Lazari-Radek, K., and P. Singer. *The Point of View of the Universe: Sidgwick and Contemporary Ethics*. Oxford: Oxford University Press, 2014.
Dennett, Daniel. *Consciousness Explained*. New York: Back Bay, 1992.
———. *Freedom Evolves*. New York: Penguin, 2003.
———. "When atheists fib to protect God." *Salon* (October 9, 2011). http://www.salon.com/2011/10/09/when_atheists_fib_to_protect_god/.
Dupre, Louis. *Passage to Modernity: An Essay in the Hermeneutics of Nature and Culture*. New Haven, CT: Yale University Press, 1993.
Eakin, Emily. "Think Tank; No Longer Alone: The Scientist Who Dared to Say Animals Think." *New York Times*, February 3, 2001.
Gadamer, Hans-Georg. *Truth and Method*. Rev. 2nd ed. Translated by J. Weinsheimer and D. Marshal. New York: Bloomsbury Academic, 2004.
Grant, Edward. *Planets, Stars and Orbs: The Medieval Cosmos, 1200–1687*. Cambridge: Cambridge University Press, 1994.
Greenway, William. *The Challenge of Evil: Grace and the Problem of Suffering*. Louisville: Westminster John Knox, 2017.
———. "Charles Taylor on Affirmation, Mutilation, and Theism: A Retrospective Reading of *Sources of the Self*." *Journal of Religion* 80/1 (January 2000) 23–40.
———. *For the Love of All Creatures: The Story of Grace in Genesis*. Grand Rapids: Eerdmans, 2015.
———. "Modern Metaphysics, Dangerous Truth, Post-Moral Ethics: The Revealing Vision of Bernard Williams." *Philosophy Today* 51 (2007) 140–54.
———. "Peter Singer, Emmanuel Levinas, Christian Agape, and the Spiritual Heart of Animal Liberation." *Journal of Animal Ethics* 5/2 (2015) 45–58.
———. *A Reasonable Belief: Why God and Faith Make Sense*. Louisville: Westminster John Knox, 2015.

Bibliography

Griffin, Donald. *Animal Minds: Beyond Cognition to Consciousness.* Chicago: University of Chicago Press, 2001.

Habermas, Jürgen. *The Philosophical Discourse of Modernity.* Translated by F. Lawrence. Cambridge, MA: The MIT Press, 1987.

Harlow, H. and Suomi, S. "Induced Psychopathology in Monkeys." *Engineering and Science* 33 (1970) 8–14.

Harris, Sam. *The Moral Landscape: How Science Can Determine Human Values.* New York: The Free Press, 2011.

Horkheimer, Max and Adorno, Theodor. *Dialectic of Enlightenment: Philosophical Fragments.* Translated by Edmund Jephcott. Redwood City, CA: Stanford University Press, 2007.

Jensen, Derrick. *A Language Older Than Words.* New York: Context, 2000.

Jonas, Hans. "Philosophical Reflections on Experimenting with Human Subjects." *Daedalus: Journal of the American Academy of Arts and Sciences* 98 (1969) 219–47.

Kane, Robert. *The Significance of Free Will.* New York: Oxford University Press, 1998.

Laplace, Pierre-Simon. *A Philosophical Essay on Probabilities.* Translated by F. W. Truscott and F. L. Emory. New York: Dover, 1951.

Lederer, Susan, E. *Subjected to Science: Human Experimentation before the Second World War.* Baltimore: The Johns Hopkins University Press, 1995.

Levinas, Immanuel. *entre-nous: On Thinking of the Other.* Translated by M. B. Smith and B. Harshav. New York: Columbia University Press, 1998.

Lightman, Alan. *The Accidental Universe: The World You Thought You Knew.* New York: Pantheon, 2014.

———. "Does God Exist?" *Salon* (October 2, 2011). http://www.salon.com/2011/10/02/how_science_and_faith_coexist/.

———. *Einstein's Dreams.* New York: Vintage Contemporaries, 2004.

———. *Mr g: A Novel About Creation.* New York: Pantheon, 2012.

———. "Why atheists should respect believers." *Salon* (October 10, 2011). http://www.salon.com/2011/10/10/atheists_believers_respect/.

Lindberg, David C. *Beginnings of Western Science.* 2nd ed. Chicago: University of Chicago Press, 2008.

Lindberg, David C., and Ronald Numbers, eds. *God and Nature: Historical Essays on the Encounter Between Christianity and Science.* Berkeley, CA: University of California Press, 1986.

Linzey, Andrew. *Animal Gospel.* Louisville: Westminster John Knox, 1998.

Linzey, Andrew, and Clair Linzey, eds. *Normalising the Unthinkable: The Ethics of Using Animals in Research.* Oxford: Oxford Centre for Animal Ethics, 2015.

McFague, Sallie. *Super, Natural Christians.* Minneapolis: Augsburg Fortress, 2000.

Rawls, John. *Political Liberalism.* New York: Columbia University Press, 1995.

———. *A Theory of Justice.* Cambridge, MA: Harvard University Press, 1971.

Ricoeur, Paul. *Hermeneutics and the Social Sciences: Essays on Language, Action and Interpretation.* Translated by J. B. Thompson. Cambridge: Cambridge University Press, 1981.

Ridley, Mark. *The Cooperative Gene.* New York: The Free Press, 2001.

Schoen, Allen. *Kindred Spirits: How the Remarkable Bond Between Humans and Animals Can Change the Way We Live.* New York: Broadway, 2002.

Schweitzer, Albert. *Out of My Life and Thought.* New York: Henry Holt, 1933.

Bibliography

Singer, Isaac Bashevis. *Collected Stories: "Gimpel the Fool" to "The Letter Writer."* New York: Library of America, 2004.

Singer, Peter. *Animal Liberation.* New York: Avon, 1975.

———. *Rethinking Life and Death: The Collapse of our Traditional Ethics.* New York: St. Martin's Griffin, 1994

Stout, Jeffrey. *Democracy and Tradition.* Princeton, NJ: Princeton University Press, 2003.

Taylor, Charles. *Sources of the Self: The Making of the Modern Identity.* Cambridge: Cambridge University Press, 1989.

Walker, Alice. *Living by the Word: Selected Writings, 1973–87.* New York: Harcourt, Brace, Jovanovich, 1988.

www.ingramcontent.com/pod-product-compliance
Lightning Source LLC
Chambersburg PA
CBHW022123160426
43197CB00009B/1138